Cordwood Construction
Best Practices

A log home building method using renewable resources and time honored techniques.

Richard Flatau

This book is dedicated to the memory of my mother, Lucille L. Flatau,
a woman of great compassion, devotion, and patience.

Cordwood Construction Resources, LLC
Merrill, Wisconsin
ISBN-13: 978-0615592701
ISBN-10: 0615592708

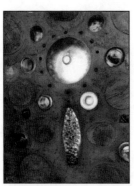

(KimAnna Cellura-Shields)

Round, round, round by Sandy Clidaras (The Cordstead Additions)

Front cover photo credit: Bryan & Lois Pratt. Back cover: Alan Stankevitz & Richard Flatau.

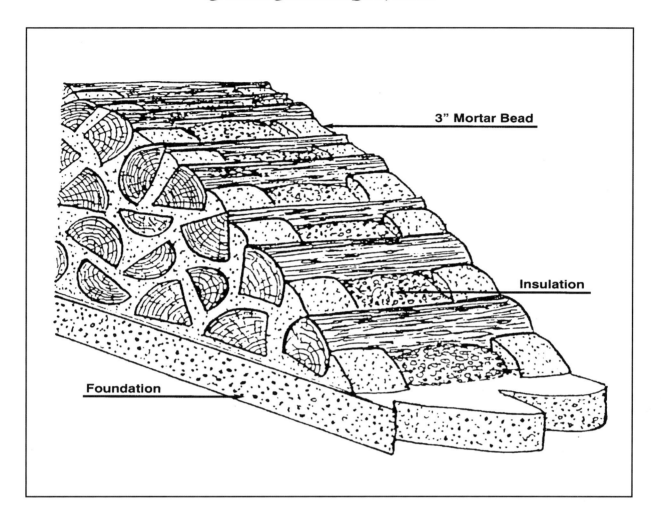

3" Mortar Bead

Insulation

Foundation

This line drawing, courtesy of the late Jack Henstridge
is unparalleled for its clear depiction of the essence of a single cordwood wall.

Definition of Cordwood Construction

*An old fashioned method of building a wall by stacking dry, peeled log ends in mortar
and insulating the center cavity to achieve maximum R-value.*

cordwood website www.daycreek.com
cordwood construction website www.cordwoodconstruction.org

Acknowledgements

Gratefulness, affection and heartfelt thanks:

To my wife Becky, who is my editor, advisor and confidant. She's the one who makes it possible for these pages to come forth with organization and clarity.   Thank you also to our delightful children Katy & Ryan who have worked on many of these cordwood projects.

To all of those wonderful folks who have been part of this journey of using alternative building methods to create unique, earth friendly structures.

Thank you for lightening the load...Many hands make light work. God speed

Table of Contents

A cordwood aviary

Author Richard Flatau and tamarack log-end ready for embedding on a cordwood building project.

Foreword

    With a critical, somewhat experienced eye this reviewer inspected and appraised the cordwood home constructed by my son and daughter-in-law. To me the simplicity of all that matters in good home building, i.e., layout, foundation, walls, trussed roof, materials and techniques employed, is done logically, "professionally" and well.

    The home is solid, modern, unique, and attractive in appearance. It augurs well for the conscientious "amateur" who has a plan, reads pertinent literature and has fortitude plus common sense. It would appear Cost-Containment, with all its attendant parameters, was achieved in a total way. At less than ten dollars ($10.00) per square foot it is truly a modern day phenomenon. It assuredly goes without the necessity for saying so; this example of what can be done (inexpensively) should encourage many to do likewise. Yes-with time, patience, and a few savings or borrowed dollars—it can be done.

H.C. Flatau, PhD, Long Beach, California
    1917-1984 Rest in peace, Dad.

Foreword

Almost all of the creatures on this Planet have the inborn ability to create their own form of adequate housing. The Human Race is no exception. If this were not true we wouldn't be here. Adequate shelter is a prerequisite to survival. Creating your own living space is "Conventional Construction."

Somewhere along the way someone came up with the idea, that rather than taking the time to do it themselves, they could hire someone else to do it for them--and thus, the housing industry was born. This should be called "Alternative" housing-not the other way around.

No one is going to build you a house out of the goodness of his or her heart. They do it because they can make money at it--it's called "profit motivation"--or what has degenerated into the "Slam-bam, thank you ma'am" technique.
Just look at the results! Homogenized designs with limited life expectancy at a cost of over one hundred thousand dollars. This is today's "conventional" housing.

If you want to save at least two-thirds of that cost, take the time and DO IT YOURSELF. It really isn't all that difficult. A great many novice builders have done it and so can you. Cordwood Construction is but one of the many house building techniques available, but it's one of the best as far as simplicity, longevity and aesthetics are concerned.

If you follow the simple directions as laid out here in Richard's book, you will not only save yourself a bundle, but will have a structure that equals or exceeds the basic building code requirements. And have the satisfaction of doing it yourself.

Jack Henstridge--Cordwood Builder,
Author, Master Mortar Stuffer
Upper Gagetown, New Brunswick
Canada

Jack left this earthly life on October 9, 2006
Rest in peace good friend...

What is Cordwood Construction?

Cordwood construction, which is sometimes called "stackwall" or "stovewood" is a form of wall building that consists of laying whole or split logs, width-wise in a bed of mortar. When looking at a cordwood wall, log ends are the only part of the wood that are visible. The wood actually rests on two mortar beds that are each about 4" thick - one mortar bed is the outside of the wall and the other bed is the inside wall. In between each bed of mortar, insulation in the form of lime treated sawdust or other insulating materials fill in the empty space between the logs and mortar. The thickness of the wall is determined by the length of the log end used. Typically, walls are anywhere from 8" to 24" thick depending upon the builder's need for energy efficiency.

Cordwood Colorado

Some builders choose to use two cordwood walls. Each wall is made up of 8" of cordwood and a layer of mortar. Insulation and a vapor barrier are sandwiched between the walls. This method makes for greater energy efficiency and less air infiltration.

History

Zachow Farmhouse 1895 Wisconsin

In the Midwest, cordwood houses started appearing with the early settlers. Old World Wisconsin, a historical village in Eagle, Wisconsin, is comprised of early settler's homes that were built throughout the state by immigrants. In the village, there is a cedar cordwood house that was built by Polish immigrants sometime in the 1880's. Their chicken coop was built right into the side of the house. This very well may be the first documented case of a cordwood chicken coop!

There are homes in Door County and the Bayfield area of Wisconsin that date back to the late 1800's. The John Mechialski Stovewood Store, built in 1899, is located in Jennings, Wisconsin. It is the first known commercial cordwood building and it happens to be a cheese factory. What else would you expect from the Dairy State?

What are the advantages of building a cordwood house?

1. **Cost** - The cost of building a cordwood house can be considerably less than a standard wood frame house. It all depends how much of the labor you can do yourself and how frugal you are in finding all of the necessary building components. After building a cordwood home myself, I learned from the experience that a person can cut building costs **in half** when compared to a standard house built by contractors. It

Cordwood House, Georgia

involves planning and labor, but the payoff comes in sweet home-owner dreams.

2. **Energy Efficiency** - Cordwood houses provide two benefits: good insulation values and thermal mass. Since the inside mortar joints are insulated from the outside wall, the mortar acts as thermal mass to keep the house at a more consistent temperature. The cordwood itself is an insulator and the density of the wood will have a slight effect on its efficiency. Sawdust or other materials fill in the cavity between the mortar beds and help insulate the walls.

   The University of Manitoba engineering department ran tests on a cordwood wall in January 2005 and reported on them in the book ***Cordwood and the Code: A Building Permit Guide.*** The engineering department tests found a 1.47 R-value per inch of cordwood wall. Therefore, a 16" cordwood wall has an R value of 24. Cliff Shockey states that a 24" (8" cordwood + 8" insulation + 8" cordwood) double wall has an R value of 40. Cliff's double wall technique is more time consuming and may require additional post and beam framing.

3. **Ecologically Friendly** - Cordwood houses use natural resources. Using sustainably harvested logs can help improve the forest. As you know, wood is a renewable resource. You can also recycle glass bottles and use them in construction of your walls. Bottle ends make for an attractive personal statement.

4. **Easy to Build** - Cordwood construction is not rocket science, but it takes time and does involve masonry. As long as you are capable of lifting and stacking logs and have some basic carpentry skills, it's not too difficult to do yourself. Just make sure that you have the necessary building code approvals ahead of time.

Double Wall Cordwood,
Alberta, Canada

5. **Satisfaction** - The Rolling Stone's couldn't find it, but with cordwood, there is a tremendous amount of satisfaction associated with building your own dwelling. Building a cordwood home makes it possible for anyone with determination and persistence, to experience the thrill of building ones own house.

6. **Fire Resistance** - In *Cordwood and the Code*, there's a good article on fire penetration and flame spread on a cordwood wall. The article discusses a real life fire that occurred when a propane-fired freezer exploded. Although the house did eventually burn, it took two days for the house to be destroyed. The insurance company, after witnessing this, dropped their insurance rates on cordwood houses finding them far superior to conventional stick frame houses.

What are the disadvantages of building a cordwood house?

1. **Time Consuming** - Building a cordwood house will take more time to build than a conventional one. How much time you devote to the project will determine how long it will take to build. Constructing a cordwood house is certainly labor intensive. But, you are making a very important trade-off: your time versus your money.

2. **Resale** - During the last 30 years, I have been aware of quite a few cordwood homes that have been bought and sold. It doesn't appear to be a problem to buy or sell a cordwood home. Lending institutions are willing to lend money for alternative construction and for purchasing alternative housing. Some of it depends on how well the home is constructed.

3. **Building Permits** The book *Cordwood and the Code: A Building Permit Guide*, which was written to coincide with the 2005 Cordwood Conference, has been a key document in obtaining a building permit. Not only does it succinctly list all the current testing data on cordwood building, but it also contains two approved building permit applications. It also comes with the Department of Energy ResCheck software and a CD to organize and compile your own building permit application.

This article is adapted and revised from a series of questions on cordwood at daycreek.com

Mermaid Cottage in Colorado. Post & beam framework, gorgeous bottle end details of the rising sun. (KimAnna Cellura-Shields)

Introduction to Cordwood Construction: Best Practices

Cordwood Construction: Best Practices comes as a result of over 30 years of experience building log end homes.   Having built my own 1600 sq. ft. cordwood home in 1979 for $15,000, I was fortunate enough to be one of a growing group of builders who were getting their 'hands dirty' with various types of alternative construction. Since then my wife and I have helped others build their cordwood homes. We have also hosted workshops, conferences and trained mortaring crews. Writing articles, consulting with cordwood home owners and being lucky enough to be involved in a few major cordwood projects, has helped me see first hand the development of cordwood in North America.

   This cordwood book is a good faith attempt to establish a set of best practices that can be used, added to and revised as the next phase of cordwood construction evolves. Professional builders and neophytes alike have offered suggestions as to how to make cordwood homes more energy efficient, sustainable and maintenance free. It is my hope that this book will guide a builder from planning stages to occupancy of a well built, energy efficient, one-of-a-kind cordwood home.

   This book will examine the following areas:

- What are some outstanding examples?
- What are current best practices with cordwood construction?
- What is the current test data on cordwood buildings?
- Where is the field of cordwood construction headed?

   All of these questions and more will be answered. A challenge will be made to encourage builders to experiment with innovations.
   Cordwood construction has grown from its "use anything, build anyway" roots into a more sophisticated method of construction.
   Cordwood Construction: Best Practices will offer state of the art examples and provide an explanation of **choices** that need to be made:

Decisions and Choices

1. Site Selection 2. Foundations 3. Framing 4. Wood species 5. Drying wood & wood prep 6. Width of wall 7. Insulation choices 8. Mortar mixes 9. Double wall or single wall	10. Roof considerations 11 HVAC (heating and air flow) 12 Design (passive solar and active solar) 13. Renewable and sustainable practices 14. Energy Star Guidelines

Interior of Flatau's Chateau with 1929 Home Comfort wood cook stove. (R. Flatau)

History   How did Cordwood get started?

Tracing the roots of cordwood construction leads one on a fascinating trail of early North American, pioneer history: From the cedar and mortar homes and barns of 18th century Quebec settlers to 1980s college-sponsored cordwood courses at the University of Manitoba, Winnipeg, Canada. Between these time lines lie homes, barns, cottages, sheds, pump houses, greenhouses and garages in New York State, New Brunswick, North Carolina, Manitoba, Alberta, Colorado, Washington, Oregon, Saskatchewan, Alabama, Minnesota, Michigan, Wisconsin, Iowa and the like. A labor intensive, sweat equity project, the cordwood home involves a maximum amount of work with a minimum amount of capital. Indeed, one may build from out of pocket funds, a wall at a time. "Why haven't I seen more of these structures?" you may ask. Many were covered during the great "clapboard siding days" of yore, some have been "stuccoed over" on the outside and drywalled on the interior. A friend (from Door County, Wisconsin) inspecting my newly completed home, remarked, "My grandfather's attic in Door County looks just like this."

The lull in cordwood building has come about for a number of reasons. It takes quite awhile to build a cordwood structure, some people don't want to be bothered with stockpiling the wood necessary for construction, and still others don't like the idea of building each wall separately. Yet, there are those who would go through any preparation necessary to realize the dream of building their own home.

Bill Tischler, University of Wisconsin-Madison Professor of Landscape Architecture, has written the most concise history of cordwood building to date and he discerns that although the real roots of cordwood construction are vague, the American cordwood boom materialized during the 1880's - 1930's when over 70 such structures were built in Wisconsin alone. The Canadian flowering occurred during the late 1800's in Quebec and New Brunswick. Many of these newly rediscovered buildings are still standing and occupied.

The Blacksmith Inn in Baileys Harbor, Door County, Wisconsin with cordwood (stovewood) wall revealed. It had been covered with lime plaster.
This Bed & Breakfast was built as a family dwelling in the late 1800's.

Although cordwood history is rather obscure, without a discernible origin and migration, the basic facts remain:

- Cordwood construction endures—some barns, homes and sheds are well over 100 years old.
- Cordwood construction is a labor intensive task, i.e., few dollars, much sweat.
- Cordwood construction takes more preparation than other techniques.
- Done properly, cordwood construction can be a ticket to a warm, pleasing, mortgage free home.
- Done improperly, cordwood construction can lead to a cold, drafty domicile.

The John Mecikalski Stovewood Store in Jennings, Wisconsin was built in 1899 and is the only known commercial stackwall building in the U.S. It was restored by the Kohler Foundation in the mid 1980's and is now used as a museum by the township. (R. Flatau)

Best Practices: A Preview

A concise review of important cordwood choices. These will be addressed in detail in the upcoming chapters.

Over the years some owner-builders in the cordwood field have continued building, writing and helping others with projects, have concluded that there are several techniques which can be labeled *Best Practices* for Cordwood Construction.

Like all building decisions there are continual cost/benefit/budget choices that must be made before and during construction. There is no absolute right way to build your home, rather there are decisions that you must make based upon available money, skills, time and preferences. When we built, one of our main goals was to come away from the project mortgage-free. Not everyone has that goal and so you adjust your purchases to meet your goals. For example, we ordered birch cabinets from JC Penny catalog for 1/5th of the cost of regular cabinets in order to meet our goal. We didn't scrimp and save on the safety issues (foundation, wiring, plumbing, chimney, furnace, windows), but we did make monetary concessions on the plumbing fixtures, floor coverings, cabinets, etc. You too, will have to make decisions based on your goals and objectives. Take the following discussion on Best Practices with that in mind.

1. **Foundations**: Most cordwood builders use an insulated frost protected shallow foundation (FPSF). Many are putting radiant-in-floor heat into the slab. It is, of course, feasible to do cordwood on a basement or crawl space, and this adds to the cost of the building. If you prefer a basement and have that as a goal, put in a basement. Remember that even with an insulated slab you can frame out the floor and put in hardwood floors. Some cordwood builders have done this and used the 2" x 6" floor framing to run electrical, plumbing and heating.

2. **Post and Beam Framing:** Most cordwood experts now agree that one of the advantages of post and beam framing, is that you can put your roof on first. That allows you to do much of the work out of the elements, it provides a covered space to store your log-ends, tools and supplies. It gives you the opportunity to build one section of wall at a time. If winter comes early, simply side up the sections that aren't finished and finish them in the spring. Even folks who have chosen the stackwall corner method are beginning to post and beam the walls in between the stackwall corners.

11.1 The Mermaid Cottage by KimAnna Cellusa-Shield is a post and beam framed cordwood beauty. This type of cabin may serve as shelter and practice building when working toward ones cordwood home. (K.Cellura-Shields)

15

3. **Wood Prep & Drying:** The biggest problem with cordwood is the natural tendency of the mortar to separate from the wood. This is why it is very important to dry your wood to the minimum moisture content (EMC) for your area.

4. **Make the walls 16 to 24 inches thick:** for optimum R-value.

5. **Cedar and other wood:** Cedar is the ideal wood for cordwood. It is light, has a good R-value, is naturally decay resistant and has a light attractive end grain. However, except for staying away from hardwoods (they have a tendency to swell and crack mortar joints) most of the other dry, insect free softwoods are suitable for cordwood building.

6. **Split some of your wood.** If you want your wood to dry faster, try splitting it. Splitting makes two things happen. The wood will dry faster and there will be no *primary check* to allow air infiltration.

7. **Mortar Mix:** The mortar mix must be one that will set up and cure slowly. There are about five basic mixes. Some will leave your walls smooth and others will have an adobe like quality. Before you make a decision it is wise to try a few of the mixes and see what they look and feel like after you mortar.

8. **Random Pattern:** Don't build with all one size wood, use a random pattern to give your cordwood building an attractive appearance. Step back from the wall every so often to see how it looks.

9. **Large Overhangs & gutters:** In order to keep the cordwood dry and free from splashback, it is a good idea to have at least a 24" overhang. It is also a advisable to gutter your roof eaves to prevent splashback.

10. **Build off the ground:** Most experts recommend that you start your cordwood at least 12 inches off the ground, however, if your climate is especially wet and humid, you will want to consult with local building officials and apply what works for your locale.

11. **Code Compliance:** One of the main thrusts of the Cordwood Conference 2005 was to establish a document that dealt with Code Issues. Fortunately the document ***Cordwood & the Code: A Building Permit Guide*** was one of the gems produced for the Conference. It has proven very successful in facilitating the 'approved' building permit.

12. **Build small now, add-on later**: Some would advise building a smaller structure now, while leaving room to add on later as more resources become available. This is one of those areas that becomes a personal decision, but it is important to know that it is an available option.

13. **Log loosening:** No matter how dry your wood is, there will most likely be some pieces that loosen up or check. This is a cosmetic problem and can be solved by applying Permachink or Log Jam caulk to the mortar around the log and stuffing the primary check.

14. Solar design: Consider passive and active solar design options. If you can't afford them right now at least keep a solar window open for later attachment.

15. Take a Workshop: Work on a cordwood project, go visit a cordwood home, and/or consult with someone who has built and lives in a cordwood home. These will be your experts.

16. Build a Practice Building: Learn the cordwood technique, gain valuable storage space, learn how to mix mortar and tuck point. This is a win/win.

11.2 Beautiful random patterning with unique wood features in, Haida Gwaii British Columbia, Canada.

11.3 A beautiful stackwall corner in Minnesota; this has been built as a complete post to fit into a post & beam framework. (R. Flatau)

Chapter 1   Owner/Builders and Experts

The section will feature the writers, builders and websites that describe cordwood construction in all its many forms. This portion also includes builders who have assisted others by writing of their progress or giving help on cordwood building sites.

Olle Hagman
Sweden
olle@kubbhus.se,   http://www.kubbhus.se
Ph.D. in Social anthropology, Göteborg University, Sweden

1.1 Olle Hanson's cordwood cabin in Sweden.

Olle used a clay based mortar for his cabin. This is how the early Swedish cordwood homes in the 1800's were built and Olle is trying to meld the old with the new.
Olle is a professor at Göteborg University in Sweden and authored two articles for the ***Cordwood Conference Papers 2011***. He also attended the Conference in Winnipeg and did a fantastic job in presenting his papers documenting the 130 cordwood buildings in Sweden and the many cordwood barns in Norway. His papers are entitled:

- *A Social History of Cordwood Houses in Sweden*
- *Norwegian Cordwood Wall Technique*

Sandy Clidaras
Log Prep & Foam Insulation

Sandy & Angelika Clidaras of Quebec have built a lovely cordwood home. They have used some effective methods of preparing their log ends and insulating between their logs with closed cell foam.

1.2 The beautiful Clidaras home in Quebec.
(Sandy Clidaras)

Sandy and Angelika's log prep, closed cell foam insulation techniques and all the other aspects of how they built their gorgeous home are available at the website listed below.
   Their Frost Protected Shallow Foundation (FPSF), log prep and insulation techniques are published in the *Continental Cordwood Papers 2005 and 2011*. They wrote two articles for each set of papers, detailing the building of their lovely home in a lake front community near Montreal, Quebec. Sandy was one of the first to use closed cell foam insulation in the center cavity of his cordwood walls. Ten years after building, he speaks of a warm, draft free cordwood home. Sandy was also an excellent Focus Group Presenter at the Cordwood Conference 2005.

*Author's note: Cordwood is a building technique that is ever evolving and improving. Even though the technique is fairly simple there are different ideas about how to accomplish the task of building a log-end wall. Sandy continues to build cordwood (a round garage and an addition, most recently) and offers a detailed summary of his **log prep, foam insulation** and considerations on **single and double wall options** on a CD of his building innovations and experiences at:*

http://thecordstead.blogspot.com/

A summary of this information is included in the Double Wall vs. Single Wall Section of this book (Chapter 9 page 96).

John Meilahn
Copper Harbor, Michigan

1.3 John Meilahn's Cordwood in the Keweenaw.

This handsome cordwood home is in the heart of the Lake Superior snowbelt. The builder John Meilahn is of proud, strong Finnish heritage. His creations shows his affinity with wood. The railing for the spiral staircase is made of ONE piece of ash (boiled and bent). The kitchen counter tops have "fall" leaves floating in a clear epoxy sealant. The shelf on the right is left open as a cat perch (and quite a good one it is).

John is a builder by trade and runs North Shore Builders in Copper Harbor with Steve Peters. He builds traditional homes and alternative construction. If you are interested in contacting John

his information is available in the Copper Harbor, Michigan phone book.

Grant Nicholson
Owen Sound, Ontario
http://www.gnicholsondesign.com/

Grant Nicholson wrote two articles for the Cordwood Conference Papers 2011. One described the "cast quions" he used for the stackwall corners on his double wall cordwood home in Owen Sound, Ontario. The other was about using a stone mason inspired "Slipform Method" for faster mortaring of cordwood walls. Grant is a designer of "signs" and an artist and as luck would have it he made a video of his slipform technique to show at the Cordwood Conference in Winnipeg on June 11-12, 2011. It was a big hit, with Grant playing acoustical guitar for musical interludes. We have been encouraging Grant to put it on Youtube. The following is the summary Grant wrote about the slipform method and his suggestions for continued improvement.

1.4 Grant Nicholson's double wall, slipformed (on the interior wall) stackwall (cordwood) creation in Ontario. Note the "cast corner quoins", the beautiful cordwood masonry, the arched door, and the four posts which will each have an inscribed pattern. The next page shows the door in detail and the patterned posts.

"In summary, the combination of cordwood and slip form was beneficial. As with most aspects of house building, timely results are achieved through excellent planning and preparation. Our use of small cedar rail stock and highway guard rails added considerable time to the project. The traditional trowel method we used on the outside of the house yielded 40 - 45 square feet of wall for every 14 single man hours, whereas slip forming produced 120 - 130 square feet of wall in the same amount of time. Applied to a double-wall process where only one side of the wall is finished the form works very well. Use of slip form to produce a single wall that is pointed on both sides is debatable; the log ends would need to be truly uniform to produce agreeable results.

One of the other advantages of slip forming is it can accommodate an unskilled worker. The form becomes your guide, ensuring a wall that is plumb and vertical. The risk of using unskilled labor comes down to accepting the size of possible large mortar joints. This may or may not be of great importance, depending on your point of view or application.

1.5 The arched doorway and rich toned, red cedar door is attached to a 24" thick, double stackwall home. The inscribed pattern on the right is repeated on all four posts that frame the entrance way.

Aesthetically, the randomized appearance of slip forming is akin to an architect's approach to buildings. A texture is created that is entirely driven by the raw materials used. The mosaic-like appearance of carefully constructed cordwood gives way to a less-contrived sense of the wood, much like aggregate within a concrete emulsion. The larger mortar joints are reminiscent of old stone barn foundations that were constructed strictly for function, almost inadvertently becoming beautiful."

Email: grant@gnicholsondesign.com
Web: www.gnicholsondesign.com
Phone Number: 1-877-470-1015
Nicholsondesign Artistic Carving & Inlay
1190 2nd Avenue East,
Owen Sound, Ontario,
Canada   N4K 2H9

NICHOLSON
D E S I G N

Author's note: Grant builds amazingly beautiful signs. A visit to his website will give you the scoop on what he builds, how he builds it and how it looks.

Bryan & Lois Pratt
Woodland Park, Colorado
http://www.infolightandliving.com/

1.5 Rocky Mountain High in Colorado.

Bryan and Lois Pratt of Colorado, visited Alan Stankevitz of daycreek.com fame in 2001. They helped Alan build walls on his cordwood home to see if cordwood was a good fit for them. After learning about the technique, they decided to build a twelve sided, two story cordwood house. They used post and beam framing and a tension/compression ring roof covered by 10" thick SIP panels with an R-Value of 40. Their engineer calculated the 18" thick cordwood walls at having an R-Value of 28… not including its thermal mass component! With this configuration, each floor is 720 square feet. The metal roof, gutters, fascia and soffit add to an almost impermeable fire retardant exterior (very important in the fire prone western forests). They used Alan's mortar recipe of :

1 part type S Hydrated lime
2 parts clay
3 parts type N masonry cement
4 parts sand
6 parts soaked paper

The paper was recycled newspaper that was shredded and soaked in water overnight then slurried with a spackle mixer until it resembled wet dryer lint. They liked the idea of using the paper for a slower drying mix in the dry Colorado air. This slower set helps strengthen the mortar.

Their home is warm and cozy, strong and sturdy. In a cold climate the combination of solar thermal and cordwood is perfect!   Bryan & Lois offer the following:

"Thermal mass and radiant heat is indeed the way to go in cold climates. The combination of cordwood masonry walls, SIP (structural insulation panel) roof and solar hot water heated floors enables us to stay warm and toasty year round, high up in the Rockies for less than 60 cents a day…and that was before we installed the photovoltaic system. After the home was complete, we added a greenhouse to an "outbuilding." This was the perfect addition to high altitude living. The 26'x16' greenhouse gave us plenty of room to grow plants all year round. Black metal barrels filled with water act as thermal mass during the cold winters. Bryan installed what is called a "subterranean" heating system. At 75 degrees, fans turn on to pull the warm air of the greenhouse into the growing beds through 4" French drain piping buried in the dirt. This prevents the dirt from freezing in the winter and moderates warmer temperatures in the summer. Four years of growing has shown us we can eat something out of the greenhouse all year round with an abundance through 3 seasons."

  Bryan and Lois run online businesses directed toward: personal health (physical, mental and spiritual), solar thermal and high altitude greenhouse gardening.

  Their website contains a wealth of information (including videos) about how they built their cordwood home. They also have an online consulting business (BnL Consulting) and offer books and videos on many health related subjects. These are people who "walk the walk." It may be worth your while to spend a little time with them online.

1.6 Interior space is very pleasing to the eye and (we are told) the view is priceless.
Contact Information:
Bryan and Lois Pratt
http://www.infolightandliving.com/
[Please leave an email message on the Contact Us portion of their interesting website.]

University of Manitoba
Dr. Kris Dick P.Eng.

The engineering department at the University of Manitoba has been building cordwood for low cost housing since the early 70's. The origin of the stackwall project was The Northern Housing Committee of the University of Manitoba's Engineering Department. The initial impetus was to find a method of building a sturdy, fire-resistant home in the rural areas of Manitoba where many fire related fatalities were occurring from poorly built, poorly insulated structures.

Dr. Kris Dick, P. Eng. is now the driving force behind stackwall building at the University of Manitoba. He also owns an alternative building/consulting business. **Building Alternatives, Inc.** Kris, in addition to conducting tests on stackwall and strawbale buildings, approves and draws plans for these types of dwellings in Ontario, Manitoba, Alberta and Saskatchewan.

Dr. Kris Dick, P.Eng
P.O. Box 22, Anola, Manitoba, Canada ROE OAO
Telephone: 204-866-3262
Website: www.buildalt.com

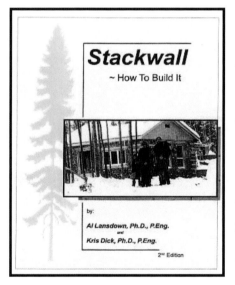

1.7 The cover of Stackwall: How to Build It, by Dr. Kris Dick and Dr. Al Lansdown.
Dr. Kris Dick, P. Eng, and his partner Dr. Al Lansdown, P. Eng. authored the book *Stackwall: How to Build It.* **The book starts with an excellent statement of purpose:**

"The whole purpose of this manual is to let you know how much work is involved in building with the Stackwall log technique (you will need some help), and to assure you that if you can acquire the materials you need for as little as we think you can, you will ultimately have an attractive, energy-conservative, fire-resistant, very reasonably priced home."

Dr. Kris Dick, P. Eng, has been an invaluable aid to cordwood and strawbale owner builders. He directed the testing of the R-value of a cordwood wall in his test facility at the Alternative Village at the University of Manitoba. The results are listed in their entirety in *Cordwood and the Code: A Building Permit Guide (2005).* The test determined that every inch of thickness of a cordwood wall (mortar, log ends, insulation) results in an R-value of 1.47. Therefore, a 16" cordwood wall has an R-value of 23.5.

"While the walls and foundations of a Stackwall building (as demonstrated in *Stackwall How to Build It*) are unusual, most other features, such as the floors, roof and trusses, are basically the same as those used in conventional housing. For these and other components, we have relied on, and refer you to, the *Canadian Wood Frame Housing Manual*, available on request from Central Mortgage and Housing Corporation in your area. (Author's note: U.S. residents might try *Wood Frame House Construction* available from the U.S. Printing Office, Washington, DC. 20402). For plumbing and wiring, consult local experts and find out from the building authority in your area what the regulations are concerning these matters."

The Stackwall manual is filled with such sage advice. It also provides invaluable formulas for determining the number of cords of wood per sq. ft. of wall, amounts of sand, lime, cement/mortar and sawdust. There is also a concise statement on choosing a building site and simple foundation layout. A discussion of types of trees to use and a unique railroad tie foundation system make this an excellent book for the novice builder looking for a quality domicile on a limited budget.

Jack Henstridge
The Grandfather of Cordwood

Jack Henstridge's book **Building the Cordwood Home** was the impetus for my dwelling, (I happened upon an ad for the book while reading his article in the *Mother Earth News*). I consider him the "Grandfather" of the cordwood movement. Jack's book is written anecdotal narrative style, with a wit, humor and wisdom that both encourages and uplifts the would-be wood-mason. His tale commences with his decision to build a traditional, horizontal log cabin after his house was destroyed by fire and traces the subsequent harrowing and surprising developments that eventually lead to his rediscovery of the cordwood method.

1.8 Jack with his Master Mortar Stuffer t-shirt and Canadian umbrella hat at the Cordwood Conference demos on July 31, 2005; his partner, Richard Flatau, is explaining how big the log ends (and fish) are in Canada.
(Ruth Ratliff)

Jack drew and bestowed his Master Mortar Stuffer certificate on those who sent him a picture of their completed building. He reckoned that you were now a member of the

ANOFAWM (Ancient and Noble Order of Free Thinking and Accredited Wood Masons). "We might have started a whole new group-complete with a secret handshake. How about a fistful of wet mortar?"-Jack Henstridge.

Jack compiled his 25+ years of building cordwood in a book called: *About Building Cordwood.* The book was an insightful and informative introduction to cordwood building. This book is currently out of print.

1.9 Master Mortar Stuffer Certificate

Authors note: Jack passed from this life on October 9, 2006. As Ross Martinek so eloquently stated, "May all modern cordwood buildings be his monument."

1.10 Jack built this turret tower at the Mother Earth News Eco-Village in North Carolina: a man with vision and whimsy. (Jack Henstridge)

Rob & Jaki Roy
Earthwood

1.11a Earthwood West Chazy, New York. (R.Flatau) Rob and Jaki Roy continue to operate Earthwood Building School in northern New York, and also spread the cordwood gospel around the world. In 2001, for example, they conducted cordwood masonry workshops in New Zealand and Chile, as well as all around the United States. They are also heavily involved in earth-sheltered housing and megalithic stone building, such as giant stone circles.

Rob and Jaki provide books, videos and classes on all these subjects and you can learn more about their work by going to:www.cordwoodmasonry.com or www.bigstones.com Or, write to Earthwood at 366 Murtagh Hill Road, West Chazy, NY 12992. Or, you can even call them and get a real human being, at 518-493-7744.

Rob has also written: *Mortage Free, Stone Circles, Timber Framing for the Rest of Us, Cordwood Building: State of the Art (2003)* and most recently *Stoneview (2007)..* He and Jaki hosted the Continental Cordwood Conference in July 1994. Rob continues to hone his craft with very fine articles in the *Cordwood Conference Papers 2005 and 2011* on *Lime Putty Mortar, New Tricks in the Cordwood Trade and Special Effects at Mushwood Cottage.* Rob & Jaki have written a travel book entitled:
The Coincidental Traveler.

1.11b This bottle end creation is a new part of Mushwood and the Cordwood Conference Papers 2011.

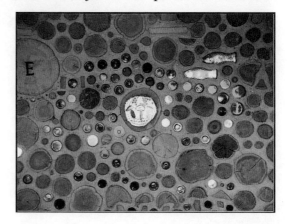

Cliff Shockey
Double Wall

Cliff Shockey has been building cordwood in western Canada since 1977. He has developed the famous, highly efficient "Double Wall Technique."

1.12 Sylvie, Becky and Summer at the Shockey homestead (R. Flatau)

Cliff won the Canadian Harrowsmith Magazine's special award for Energy Efficiency in 1993. He is not only an excellent builder, but an excellent human being. Cliff sold his organic Saskatoon Berry Farm and he continues to help others learn how to build double wall cordwood. He put an addition onto his first cordwood home and is busy with projects like his pyramid greenhouse. His book is a very worthwhile read for anyone, but especially for those planning to build in cold climates or considering the double wall technique. With air infiltration being a major post-erection headache with cordwood, Cliff's ideas will give you a warm, draft free dwelling.

1.13 Cliff in front of the double wall Shockey Insurance Building in Vanscoy, SK, Canada. (R.Flatau)

Cliff's well written and profusely illustrated book ***Stackwall Construction: Double Wall Technique*** (now in a

revised edition) is available in the ordering section at the end of this book.

Cliff Shockey
Box 193
Vanscoy, Saskatchewan
CANADA S0L 3JO   Phone: 1-306-668-2141

Alan Stankevitz
Double Wall, Post & Beam, Open Cell Foam

Alan Stankevitz of La Crescent, Minnesota has been an active participant in the cordwood movement. He has developed the much visited Daycreek.com website. Daycreek.com has become the clearing house when it comes to "all things cordwood." Alan's website has an active reader participation Forum, in which readers can ask and answer questions and a *Meet the Masons* section where people who have built using cordwood give a brief overview of their project. A section entitled *Cordicles* (Cordwood Articles) allows readers a visit to many of the articles published in Mother Earth News, Backhome Magazine, Home Power and various newspapers and state historical journals on cordwood. Alan has a comprehensive section titled *All Things Cordwood* and links to other cordwood websites. One of my favorite parts of daycreek.com is the Journal. Alan has posted to his Journal quite often and most of the time he includes his research, so you get the gist of how and why he made the decision he made. The caveat is he codes every entry in "pun speak" so the entry on solar energy might have "Snap, Crackle and Pop" as the title. Forewarned is forearmed.

Needless to say, it is worth a few minutes of your time to visit this intriguing, well put together website. It would also be appropriate to mention that Alan has installed a 4.2 KW photovoltaic array and also solar hot water panels for radiant-in-floor heat. His www.daycreek.com Journal gives all the details of Alan & Jo's cordwood journey that began in 1999 and continues to this day.

1.14 This photo gives you an idea of the renewable energy being utilized at the Stankevitz homestead. 4.2 KW photovoltaic system and five 4' x 10' solar hot thermal hot water/glycol collectors. These collectors heat his domestic hot water, his radiant in floor heat and his insulated sand bed. (A. Stankevitz)

www.daycreek.com

Wayne Higgins   G & P Beveridge
Keeweenaw Peninsula, Michigan

1.15 Wayne & Marlys Higgins gorgeous cordwood work of art, in Calumet, Michigan.

Wayne has helped foster a very unique and exciting cordwood community in the Copper Country of Michigan's Upper Peninsula. His home is usually the first that people interested in cordwood come to see. It is right off the highway that runs along the Western shore of Lake Superior. Wayne is always ready with a hot cup of coffee and a story or two to entertain the visitor. He is also an excellent tour guide and he knows the history of the area. Wayne first introduced us to the Beveridge's (right)

1.16 This is the two story creation (Camp Cordwood) of Copper Country residents, George & Paulette Beveridge. It has so many fine and interesting wood components that it could qualify as the Disneyland of Cordwood.

Scot Runyan
How to become Rent & Mortgage Free
http://rentandmortgagefree.intuitwebsites.com/

Scott wrote the book *How to Become Rent & Mortgage* Free back in 1984 and has also revised and updated his strategy that directs people to becoming a home owner without a mortgage. He has since developed a website, fostered a newsletter and is building what his friends term The Taj Mahal (an 8,000 sq. ft. cordwood mansion). The quickest way to access Scot's information is to go to his website and sign up for his eNewsletter (see address above)

Scot made this cost saving comparison of a stick built wall vs. a cordwood with all current cost calculations.

Cordwood wall cost comparison

Stick Frame	Cordwood
32' x 40' One-story home = 1,280 sq. ft.	32' x 40' One-story home = 1,280 sq. ft.
• 144 linear feet of wall 8' high = 1,152 sq ft of surface	• CMU Block Post and Beam
• 1,152 sq ft of sheet rock hung, taped and textured @ 1.30 sq ft = $1,497	• 914 CMU Blocks to build the 20 columns & bond beam @ $1.25 each = $1,142
• 1,152 sq ft interior prime & painting @.50 sq ft = $576	• 1,274 linear ft of #5 Rebar @ .45 per ft = $573
• 1,152 sq ft of "Hardy plank siding" @ $5.00 sq ft = $5,760.	• 7.5 yards of Grout @ $100. per yard = $750
• 1,152 sq ft of exterior painting @ .50 sq ft = $576	• Pump truck $350
• 1,152 sq ft of R-19 fiberglass batt insulation @ .90 sq ft = $1,036	• 3 yards of mortar @ $100. yd = $300
• 1,152 sq ft of stick framed lumber @ 3.25 sq ft = $3,744	• 5 cords of Cedar @ $150. per cord = $750
• 1,152 sq ft of OSB sheething @ .50 sq ft = $576	• Foam Insulation $250.
	• Rebar Positioning Guides $50
• 1,152sq ft of TYVEK @ .25 sq ft = $288	• 1 yard sawdust chips for mortar $100
Total cost of materials and skilled labor =$14,053	**Total cost of materials only, no labor =$4,265**

Data compiled by Scot Runyan

Tom Huber
Stone and Cordwood

***1.17   Tom & Holly Huber built this stone & wood lodge in Watervliet, Michigan.
(T.Huber)***

Tom Huber has been writing, dreaming and building with stone and wood for many a year   Tom has a love of Hobbit-Folk Architecture and a special knack of fitting the wood, stone and glass into almost magical combinations. The effects of his construction are pleasing to the eye and the spirit. Tom is a college administrator and an advocate for an environmentally friendly way of life. He has written articles for the 1999, the 2005 and *2011* **Continental Cordwood Conference Papers.**

Tom and Holly sold their cordwood homestead in southwestern western Michigan (see picture above). Tom took a new position at Paul Smith's College in upstate New York. Their wonderful home and property sold quickly. Tom confided that all the buyers were especially "taken" by the stone and cordwood. So instead of being a deterrent to selling, it was actually a huge asset.   Tom continues to write, hike, camp and dream about all the possibilities that the natural environment and green building have to offer ourselves and our planet.

As usual Tom has an engaging mind and an active body. On the following page is his latest cordwood creation. He built this after he built his super chicken coop nearby. Tom is experimenting with CEM (Cellulose Enhanced Mortar) and his current formula is in the later section on Mortar Mixes.

1.18 Tom Huber's cordwood cabin in the Adirondack's in upstate New York. As you can see Tom builds beautifully with stone, wood and mortar.

1.19 A close-up example of Tom's panache with stone, mortar, cordwood and glass, built while he sojourned in Michigan. In addition to being a thoughtful gentleman, he has a serious handyman skill set. (T. Huber)

From this brief review of some of the significant builders and writers in the field of cordwood construction, this discourse will now delve into: Best Practices, Site Selection, Foundations, Framing, Wood Species, Drying Wood and Wood Preparation, Width of Wall, Insulation Choices, Mortar mixes, Double Wall or Single Wall, Roof Options, HVAC (heating and air flow), Design (passive solar and active solar), Renewable and Sustainable Practices, Energy Star Guidelines, a Cordwood Photo Album with color photos, a Recommend Reading List, a description of the Best Practices with cordwood, how to become Mortgage-Free, Cordwood Siding Continental Cordwood Conference Summaries 2005 and 2011, Cordwood Cabin (a condensed version), White Earth Reservation Cordwood Home, the original Mother Earth News article "Mortgage Free with Cordwood Construction," ordering information and much, much more.

1.20 A beautiful picture of a stackwall corner. Note the stone foundation and fiberglass batt insulation. The blocks are 30" long 6" x 6"s. (B. Gormley)

Site Selection & Pattern Language

The most important decision a home builder can make is where to "site" the residence. This should be done with careful consideration and without haste. Wind direction, solar window, drainage, landscape, seasonal changes, view, ease of access should all be taken into consideration, before a shovelful of dirt is turned. The best book, in my humble opinion, for site selection and building ideas is Christopher Alexander's **A Pattern Language.**

Even though this book is written by an architect, it still holds to a common sense approach that an individual, with some careful observation, can design a home that best fits his/her needs in an environmentally friendly, person friendly manner.

According to Alexander his work originated from an observation that:

"At the core... is the idea that people should design for themselves their own houses, streets and communities. This idea... comes simply from the observation that most of the wonderful places of the world were not made by architects but by the people".
—Christopher Alexander, **A Pattern Language.**

The book uses words and assigns numbers to describe patterns, supported by drawings, photographs and charts. It describes exact methods for constructing practical, safe, and attractive designs at every scale, from entire regions, through cities, neighborhoods, gardens, buildings, rooms, built-in furniture, and fixtures down to the level of doorknobs. The patterns are regarded by the authors not as infallible..."

This from Alexander's website: "If you are a landowner, this website can show you ways of working that are more capable of creating healthy, hospitable and beautiful places for people to live, than present forms of practice typically allow. It does not cost more."
http://www.livingneighborhoods.org/

Site selection is such an individualized choice that only a few basic, common sense fundamentals need be observed. Remember, there's no moving the house once the foundation is in place, so choose your spot wisely:

1. The site must have good drainage. There should be no standing water at any time of the year—especially in the spring.

2. A soil sample (below the topsoil) should be taken. Your local or state agricultural or soil conservation office will do this for free or a nominal fee.

3. Have an experienced local contractor check your land for potential building sites. This may be the best way of determining a viable site, as the experienced local contractor will

have knowledge of the soil problems and conditions in your area. Ask questions!

4. Check with your county zoning commission to determine what zoning ordinances apply, i.e., what type of septic system must you install, do you need a percolation test? A percolation test is a test to determine how fast water will drain through your soil; it must drain at minimal rate in order to be suitable for a septic drain field; the alternative is an expensive holding tank which must be pumped on a regular basis. How about a well? How far must it be from the septic drain field? How far must your home be offset from the road? How far must your home be from the other property lines, power lines, lakes, rivers, etc.? How far will the power company come in if you desire electricity? What about maintenance of your road? What building codes apply to you? Will you be allowed to do your own plumbing, wiring and foundation or, by state statute, must it be done and/or inspected by a certified master of the craft involved? Yes, it sounds frightening, all these rules, laws and regulations. It sure was easier to build 20 years or 50 years ago, but if you have a strong desire to build you must make yourself knowledgeable of all that pertains to your projected home. And take it from a novice—you can do it, if you take the time to read and ask questions.

5. Check the site for slopes, trees, position of the sun (especially if you plan to use solar now or in the future), possible garden sites, (it's tough to go 400 yards to get onions and tomatoes while the soy-burgers are burning on the grill), outbuildings, fencing, etc.

6. Read Christopher Alexander's book, ***A Pattern Language.***

7. Next, drive four painted stakes at your approximate house site and square the corners; that is, set them up so that you have a perfect square or rectangle. To do this lay out a triangle at each corner using multiples of 4-5-3. When you have the corners set up and the length and width determined, then measure the diagonals from opposite corners. If the measurements are equal, you have four square corners. Do not use a string that stretches or you will have inaccurate measurements. This set of strings gives a good idea of the size of your house and you should make changes now.

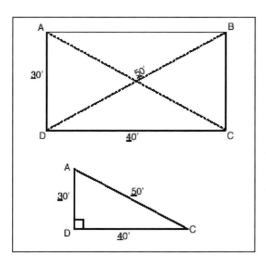

1.21 Make each corner a right angle triangle using the 4-5-3 rule. Then measure the diagonals AC and BD to insure square-ness.

Chapter 2 Foundation Options

There are a number of ways to approach the foundation question. Some people know exactly what they want. Others want the most effective, lowest cost foundation possible; yet others are simply exploring all the options. So, let's explore the possibilities:

1. **Basement/Crawl Space**—Some people want a basement. If you have the money, skills and proper site this can be an effective foundation option. However, basements cost the most of any foundation. So it is wise to explore all the possibilities if you are interested in cost effectiveness. . For those who worry about where the furnace and hot water heater will be located, there are ways to place all the mechanical systems on the first floor. However, if you need or want a basement here is one example of how to do it with cordwood.

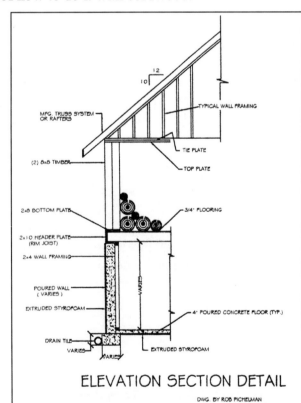

ELEVATION SECTION DETAIL

DWG. BY ROB PICHELMAN

2.1 (Above) A full walk-out basement, post and beam framed cordwood home.

2.2 (Left)This is a side section detailing one way to do cordwood on a basement. Notice that the basement is capped with a floor. The floor is braced to withstand the weight load of the cordwood walls (approximately 500 pounds per lineal foot) and the roof load. The basement walls are strengthened and there is an interior bearing plate for the floor joists. When contemplating a basement with cordwood walls make certain to plan for the extra weight.

. This basement foundation is a poured 10" concrete wall. There is a central bearing beam running down the middle of the basement. A wooden floor was put on top of the basement, before the cordwood was laid up. The structure of the floor was made of I-Joists (which are stronger than dimensional lumber) spaced 12" on center. All this is explained in detail in the article *Cordwood on a Basement* in the *Cordwood Conference Papers 2005.*

Basements are expensive to build. We put up the entire shell of our home for what it would have cost to erect the basement. Ken Kern, advocate of the owner-built home, deduces that 10-20% more living area per dollar can be built above ground than below. Since this is not a debate for or against crawl spaces or basements, let's conclude that the crawl space or basement is a viable option for the cordwood builder, and yes, people have built cordwood homes with each.

A crawl space is basically a reduced height basement without a poured floor. It is usually used in areas that have a shallow frost line.

2.3 Cordwood on a crawl space. This beautiful cordwood cabin in Houghton, Michigan was completed by the Barna family. It uses a crawl space as its foundation.
The construction of the crawl space is documented in the article; My Cordwood Dorm Room in the Cordwood Conference Papers 2005.

2. Pressure Treated Wooden Basement

There is a method of building a basement using pressure treated lumber. The picture below shows the result. There is footer poured first nd then a 2" x 10" pressure treated framework is erected. Pressure treated plywood is attached to the exterior of the framework. There is a floor placed on top of the framework (beefed up similar to the poured concrete basement).   The interior walls are insulated and sided or dry-walled. The cordwood is built on top of the capped basement. It is important to have good drainage and waterproof the sidewalls. .

The pressure treated wooden basement to the left has been in place for over twenty years and is structurally sound. When using pressure treated lumber use the non-toxic kind.

2.4 The Prange home with a pressure-treated lumber basement, a 24' x 24' cordwood addition and a truss room-in-the-attic. (R. Prange)

39

3. Frost Protected Shallow Foundation (FPSF)

A slab foundation becomes both the foundation and the floor in a typical cordwood home; so you are getting two functions for the price of one. The main idea behind the floating slab is not just cost-effectiveness, but the slab's ability to "float" if any movement does occur and hence the building will not be damaged or cracked by soil settling or earth shifting. My own cordwood home is built on a turned-edge floating slab and I have had no problem, whatsoever, with frost heaving or movement of the foundation.

Frank Lloyd Wright used a foundation enhancement in Wisconsin. He called it a "Rubble Trench Foundation." He suggested to go below the frost line with a trench of medium sized stone that would be tamped-down, between the drain tile and where the bottom edge of the concrete will form. He discusses his foundation in *The Natural House* (New York, Horizon Press, 1954). The following diagram is an updated version of the Rubble Trench Foundation. It can be used with the Frost Protected Shallow Foundation (FPSF) uses extruded Styrofoam as insulation.

2.5 The rubble trench and FPSF (frost protected shallow foundation) used at the Cordwood Education Center in Merrill, Wisconsin. (R. Cox)

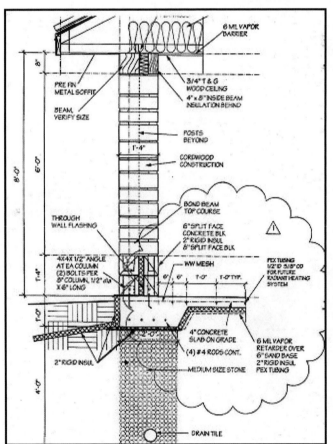

This foundation is much simpler and cheaper to build when compared to a conventional basement foundation. There are over five million of these in use in Scandinavia. These are now approved as an effective foundation in North America (www.NAHB). It is important to insulate the slab on all sides, underneath and away from the foundation for Passive Annual Heat Storage (PAHS).

One of the best books on foundations is: *Foundations and Concrete Work* by Fine Homebuilding. Taunton Press.

www.taunton.com

The following diagram is courtesy of Grant Nicholson of Owen Sound, Ontario. It shows another method of insulating a FPSF when double wall cordwood is used. This effectively provides a foundation that has no energy nosebleed.

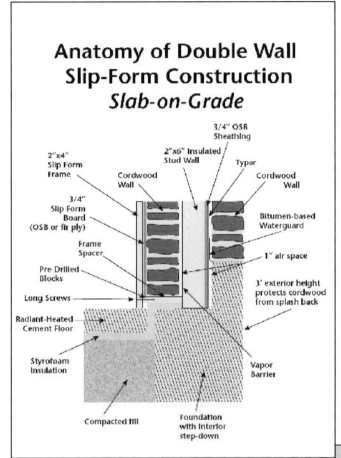

2.6 This line drawing by Grant Nicholson of Ontario shows a double cordwood wall with a slab on grade foundation. Grant also mortared on the inside wall with a slipform technique (similar to what is used for a rock wall) with cordwood. He writes about it in his article entitled: **Slipform and Cordwood** *in the Cordwood Conference Papers 2011.*

2.7 A frost protected shallow foundation (FPSF) with insulation positioned to stop typical energy nosebleed where cordwood meets the slab.

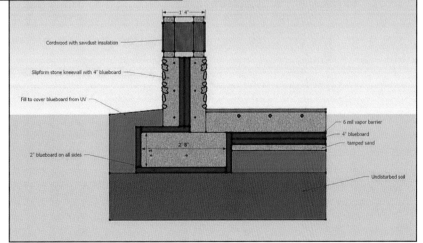

Setting your cordwood off of the foundation is a good idea in most any climate. It will keep the cordwood away from 'splashback', like snow and rain.

2.8 This picture from Julie Dale shows how a block is used as a splashback guard. These stackwall corners are actually bolted to each other so they form a post.

Notice there are two blocks (look at the blocks on the right) set on the concrete floor. The one to the outside is a thin "faced" block that looks like granite and the one to the inside is a regular-size 'split face' block. To prevent an "energy nosebleed" a 2" piece of Styrofoam is positioned between them. The cores of the block are also filled with insulation. This set up is for a garage with 12" walls. The posts are two pressure treated 6" x 6"s. The corners are stackwall (one could just as easily put posts at the corners). Note that the post on the left has been vertically "keyed" with two 1"x 2"s to hold the mortar. The Frost Protected Shallow Foundation (FPSF) is insulated underneath and around the perimeter.

4. ICF's or Insulated Concrete Forms—When Joe Nagan (Wisconsin Energy Star Director) gave his presentation at the *Cordwood Conference 2005* on cordwood and the code, he mentioned that the combination of an ICF foundation and cordwood was a "slam dunk" building combination.*(The following excerpt is from **Sandy Clidaras** who built his cordwood home and garage using the ICF system as a foundation.)* "Having decided on a Frost Protected Shallow Foundation (FPSF) system, we next thought of how we were going to form it up. We considered the following:

- It is imperative to insulate the foundation from exterior elements.
- ICF's are versatile for shapes (curves, rounds, angles etc.) and sizes, (wall thickness).
- ICF's are easy to install, lightweight & stack like giant Legos.

- ICF's save time since they are installed once and left in place.
- ICF's can save you money, if they are installed by the owner-builder.
- ICF systems accommodate to fasten "finishing" on exposed surfaces.
- ICF's are more readily accepted by building inspectors.
- ICF's accommodate steel rebar reinforcement (supports)
- If used to install a short stem wall, (to keep the logs up off of the ground), the footing & stem wall can be poured all at once creating a very strong foundation.

2.9 Sandy Clidaras' ICF foundation and stem wall forms.

Foundation penetrations should be accurately located and installed in the ICFS. Doorways need to be cut back and the form end blocked and braced. Well water supply pipe, main drain pipe, underground electrical wiring (to shed, driveway lamps etc.), future building extensions, future plumbing or electrical access entry, satellite or cable TV, phone lines, etc. It's better to have a spare opening (as simple as an ABS pipe in the form) available than to have to install one in such a wide concrete foundation later. Various ICFS companies use different stacking and bracing systems, so it's best to consult & deal with someone locally in case you need assistance, or to pick up some missing item during the assembly. A full copy of FPSF & ICFS Basics is available at the *Research Corner* on our web site.

http://thecordstead.blogspot.com/

Another helpful website Portland Cement Association *www.cement.org*

Weight of a Cordwood Wall

Weight becomes an important topic when figuring out how "stout" to make your foundation. Remember that a typical slab uses 3000 pound concrete, this means 3000 pounds per square inch before failure. The condition of the subsoil (clay, sand, gravel, etc.) becomes far more important than the concrete footing or slab.

According to the University of Manitoba's book *Stackwall: How to Build It* "A 24 inch thick cordwood wall weighs approximately 500 pounds per lineal foot." After much discussion with Rob Roy and Alan Stankevitz, it has become clear that due to the many variables involved in a cordwood wall (species of wood, weight of insulative material, thickness of mortar bead, ratio of wood to mortar, thickness of cordwood wall, etc.) there is need to define a "range of weight." We therefore offer the following conclusion: *A cordwood wall weighs approximately 30-60 pounds per cubic foot (PCF) depending on the variables listed above.*

Chapter 3   Framing (wall types)

Determining which framing system to use:

---

1. **Post and Beam**

2. **Stackwall**

3. **Round** (with or without posts)

4. **Double Wall**

Each framing style has its special considerations and uses. The final decision must be one that considers one's likes, dislikes, finances and abilities. Let's discuss each one:

1. Post and Beam—This was my original choice for a number of reasons; the rugged appearing, sturdy framework of an earlier era lent a definite pioneer quality to the all important "look" of the structure. The posts would be easily selected from the straightest and soundest cedar in my 14 cord collection (I used 32 posts and beams for framing and door and window placement). The posts were sawed on two opposite, parallel sides, so that the cordwood could come flush to the beams. The posts are cut and leveled (using shims) and then anchor bolted to the slab, the top plate is then secured. Always double check for "levelness and squareness" as you proceed and be sure to cross-brace your building.

3.1 A Post and Beam framework is very simple carpentry. These posts are secured to the slab using anchor sleeves and ¼" angle iron metal brackets.

A much relished advantage of the post and beam framework is that one could work with, and complete an 8'x 8' section of wall in two full (10 hr) work days (i.e. two people working moderately or one person working feverishly). If you have friends or relatives who become interested in cordwood, invite them over for work days.

3.2 (Left) With a post and beam framework it is of the greatest importance to keep everything braced and cross braced. If you don't, things will move and you will find yourself out of "plumb."

Post and beam is a much simpler form of Timber Frame Construction. Timber Framing involves notching, mortise, tenons, and heavy equipment (or lots of strong bodies) for lifting and setting timbers. Post and Beam can utilize dimensional lumber (2" x 12"s, 2" x 10"s, etc.) for the top and bottom plates. Dry softwood posts and beams are actually quite manageable.

When handling the large posts it is useful to have help. One important consideration is to "double level" each post, diagonally brace each corner and check the hypotenuse (using the 3'-4'-5' rule). A beginning carpenter can easily frame a building by carefully checking all measurements and keeping everything square. The posts can be trimmed on the two parallel cordwood sides leaving the exposed inner and outer side with a rounded edge. Don't square the posts on all four sides unless that is your desire. The rounded inner and outer edge are pleasing to the eye.

3.3 A 'happy hybrid' framing combo: Stackwall corners with a double post and beam framework to accommodate 16" cordwood walls. The Stackwall corners are actually bolted together to make a sturdy post. (R. Flatau)

Metal brackets *(Bruce Kilgore photo credit)*

"Post and beaming" can also be done with dimensional lumber, nails, screws and plates. For those who have chosen the post and beam method but can't find enough big posts, consider taking two smaller posts, have them rough-cut square on 3 sides, butt them together and join with 2" x 6"s or truss plates.

Rob Roy's book *Timber Framing for the Rest of Us* is a valuable resource for understanding simple methods of framing with metal fasteners and brackets. See the ordering section at the end of the book for more information.

Using wood from your own Woodlot

In Wisconsin, where I hail from, it was considered a "no-no" to use lumber from your own land for structural building purposes. However, the Department of Commerce, Division of Buildings & Safety, provided a way for landowners to use their own, "native sawn, ungraded lumber." The Wisconsin Uniform Dwelling Code (UDC) has a "commentary" built into the code, whereby, the code officials, in discussion with experts, interpret and comment on various concerns and solutions to problems that have been raised by the public. In this case, landowner's wanted to use their own woodlot to cut materials to build their homes. Until this commentary, they were in violation of the law if they used native sawn, ungraded structural lumber. [Other states, like New York, let the local sawyers 'grade' the native sawn lumber. Minnesota requires a pressure treated structural member on the exterior of the building. Check your state and local codes.]

The following commentary, used with permission, is from the Wisconsin State website, Department of Commerce, Division of Buildings and Safety. It offers a brief explanation of how the problem was resolved. (Comm 21.02, page 16).

www.legis.state.wi.us/rsb/code/

---

3. Native Sawn Ungraded Lumber

Sound native sawn un-graded lumber may be used for one and two-family dwellings Using method (1a) or (1b) below to determine allowable design stresses at 19 percent moisture content.

(1a) The native sawn lumber must be graded and certified in accordance with nationally recognized lumber grading rules for visually graded lumber per ASTM D245. Agencies publishing grading rules are listed in the NDS "Design Values for Wood Construction."

(1b) Alternative Method – Use the NDS published allowable design stresses for the lumber species using No. 3 utility grade for studs, rafters, and joists and No. 1 grade for beams, stringers, post and timbers in lieu of certified lumber graders.

Wisconsin recently implemented a new method to encourage the use of wood from one's own woodlot. An interested person "must attend one of the Wisconsin Local-Use *Dimension Lumber Grading Short-Courses* that are offered. These one day special short-course training sessions are offered several times a year, at no charge, and are advertised in the WI-DNR's *Wisconsin Woods Marketing Bulletin*."

46

Anchoring the Posts to the Slab

3.4 The posts are anchored to the insulated, floating slab with angle iron bolted to the

slab and lag screwed to the frame. Make sure there is a damp proof shingle under the post. These posts are squared on two sides. The cordwood infill will be 16". (R.Flatau)

Some people will use a pressure treated, bottom sill plate to attach the posts The posts are then secured to the bottom plate with screws, angle iron or nails. Other people like to drill a hole and then place an "anchor sleeve" in the hole. This anchor sleeve receives a bolt which then flares out the bottom of the anchor sleeve under the slab. The angle iron has holes drilled in it and is bolted to the slab and lag screwed to the post. See Addendum 2 for detailed information on bolting the posts to the slab. <u>Remember to place a damp proof material (ice & water shield or a shingle) under the post, so moisture will not wick up and rot the post.</u>

Post and beam drawings.

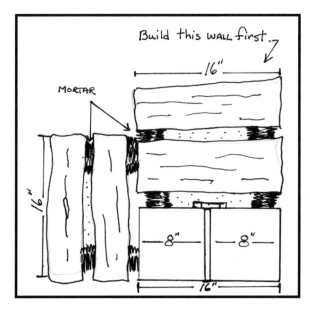

Build this WALL first.

16"

MORTAR

16"

8"   8"

16"

When planning your walls, be sure and get out pencil and paper and draw where you think your posts will be placed. Pretend you are looking down at your wall from **up in the air** (called "top view" for the professionals out there).

3.5 Some folks might use four 8" x 8" posts in this situation, but it would save materials by only using two posts. It will be important to know what the stress loads are for the posts (i.e. how much weight they will support). (R.Flatau)

47

2. Stackwall

The University of Manitoba is responsible for this effective technique of cordwood construction. As the accompanying diagram indicates the corners are first built up with rough sawn 8"x 8"s (30 inches long). Then a corner clip and mason's line are set between each set of opposing blocks and the walls are then built square and level. One of the distinct advantages of this method is that the walls can be any thickness, from 8" to 36", depending on the builder's dreams and schemes. Professional masons are already equipped with all the proper tools for this technique and they may be worth consulting for helpful hints on using corner clips, levels, plumb bobs, trowels and cement mixers. The detailed diagram, courtesy of the University of Manitoba's Engineering Department, is worth 10,000 words on the subject.

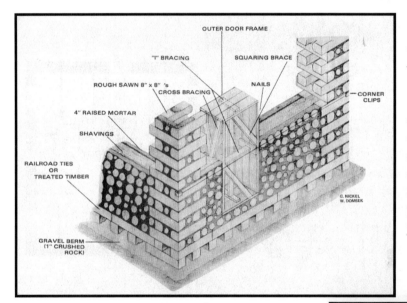

3.6 **The *Stackwall Method (Courtesy of the University of Manitoba).* The corner clips hold mason's line that helps keep the wall straight and level. This is a good example of how the railroad tie foundation works. Available from *www.buildalt.com***

3.7 **Stackwall corners around a timber frame in Custer, Wisconsin. Note the rock foundation and the window box at the far right. The timbers are 8" x 8" x 18' and the 'bents' add strength and stability. These are 'faux' stackwall corners and are not load bearing.   (R. Flatau)**

3.8 Stackwall corners in Nicole Barna's dorm room; built with her family the summer before her freshman year of college. (R. Flatau)

3. Round

Many owner/builders have built round cordwood homes in our age of perpendiculars, right angles and squares. The round structures have a sense of antiquity-Romanesque architecture—and gaiety; something the child in each of us loves. The many round cordwood buildings and other towers and turrets built by Jack Henstridge with cordwood are the finest examples I know, and represent a new era/old era blending that initially impresses one's sense of "taste" and consequently uplifts one's "spirit".

The main enigma of the round house, for me, is the 'Roof.' My novice carpentry skills are a bit aghast at tackling all those angles and degrees that go hand in hand with a round roof. Perhaps it would be worth it to live in a "circle." You decide.

The walls are built in the same manner as a curved wall home and Figure 3.9 shows a fine example of design possibilities in round cordwood homes. With Post and Beam the builder may choose to put the roof on before the walls go up; with round you must mortar from door jam to door jam before you put your roof on, unless you choose Round-Post and Beam.

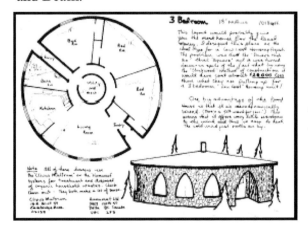

3.9 Jack Henstridge's round 3 bedroom house design. (Jack Henstridge)

3.10 A Round-Post & Beam home by Jim Coonen, Merrill, Wisconsin. Building round, within a post & beam framework, is an excellent way to get your roof on first and then infill with cordwood section by section. (R. Flatau)

3.11 Jessi & Dan Peterson used a post and beam framework for their almost round home in Wisconsin. They topped it with a living roof.

Once your foundation is in place, your wood is cut and drying and your wall style is chosen, you are almost ready to begin the challenge of laying up a cordwood wall.

No matter what method you have chosen, you need to locate doorways, windows, electrical receptacles, vents, furnace vents, plumbing inlets-outlets and any other openings you've devised in your house plans. Using graph paper to layout the house, doors, rooms, windows, lights, etc. is an important part of the building process. Do not try and make these decisions as the shell goes up. Move things around to suit your fancy on paper. Study other homes and floor plans to obtain the best possible layout for your building footage.

4. Double Wall by Cliff Shockey

Cliff invented the double wall technique in 1977 as he was building his first cordwood home in the cold Canadian Prairie town of Vanscoy, Saskatchewan. He won a Harrowsmith Magazine award for energy efficiency and has since been spreading the good news of double wall to interested persons. The wall consists of an 8" cordwood wall on the outside, 10" of rigid fiberglass in the middle and 8" of cordwood on the inside. There is a vapor barrier between the fiberglass and the inside wall.

Cliff's home is warm and toasty in the winter, due to the fact that he faced it south, put large overhanging shutters on the windows, has no windows on the north, insulated the heck out of his roof, installed radiant in-floor heat and used the double wall cordwood technique.

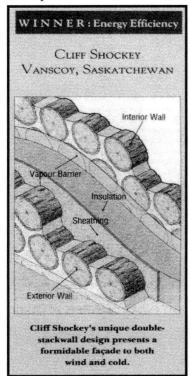

3.12 Here is a picture of Cliff's double wall as it was drawn by Harrowsmith Magazine's art department.

3.13 A photo of the double wall master putting up his sauna. Note: the mason's line running horizontal to the work. (C. Shockey)

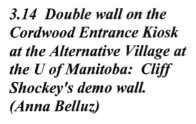

3.14 Double wall on the Cordwood Entrance Kiosk at the Alternative Village at the U of Manitoba: Cliff Shockey's demo wall. (Anna Belluz)

3.15a Here are four double wall cordwood homes.   Most of these have been built with inspiration from Cliff Shockey

Clockwise from top left: Booth's Toivola, Michigan; Shockey's, Saskatchewan, Canada; Stankevitz's La Crescent, MN, Kilgore's, New York.

3.15b Cliff Shockey demonstrates the building of the inside of a double wall building at the Cordwood Conference 2011 in Winnipeg. Note the outside stackwall, the middle rigid insulation and the interior 8" cordwood. There is also a masons line near Cliff's yellow glove. This mason's line helps keep the wall straight and cordwood rounds level.

3.14c Alan Stankevitz's two story, double wall cordwood home on the inside. Note that the walls are a little over 16 feet tall. They are post framed with cedar. The joists tie into a central column and there is a bedroom and utility space on the second floor. Alan made the home handicapped accessible and all the main functions are on the first floor. The stove is a Hearthstone soapstone woodstove, which is for cloudy days when the solar radiant in floor heat needs a wee bit of help. (R.Flatau)

Chapter 4   Wood Choices
Types of Wood for Cordwood

Choosing the type of wood to use in your cordwood structure is another individual decision since there are, once again, numerous alternatives. A decay-resistant softwood would be the most suitable. Softwoods are highly prized for cordwood. They are light, have higher insulation values than hardwood and don't swell and crack mortar joints (like hardwoods).

In this category, the most ideal decay resistant woods are:

Catalpa
Cedar   (Cedar is the gold standard for cordwood in the north)
Cypress

A little farther along the decay resistant spectrum is:

Tamarack (Tamarack acts more like a hardwood and is best used for posts & paneling)
Douglas Fir
White Pine
Red Pine
Spruce
Locust* (very decay resistant and hard)
Sassafras*

Then come:

Aspen*   (a hardwood that "acts" like a softwood)
Basswood*
Lodgepole Pine

(*Hardwoods have a tendency to swell and crack mortar joints.)

I believe it is wise to avoid using hardwoods like elm, birch and alder since they have a tendency to become develop rot. Jack Henstridge had advocated using whatever you have at hand and Rob Roy has experimented with using hardwoods. Rob found that hardwoods have a tendency to swell and crack mortar joints. He attempted to make the bottom section of Earthwood out of very dry hardwoods. After a downpour, they took on so much moisture that they actually pushed the wall out of plumb. He replaced the cordwood with cement block.

The final decision boils down to "what's available," how much does one need and what are the local resources. As to locating the best cordwood species in your area, contact your forestry agent or local loggers.   Putting an ad in the paper for a specific kind of wood should provide a quick answer to what wood is available and how much it will cost per cord. Of course if you're lucky enough to have your own woodlot, or you can barter for your materials, so much the better.

Types of Wood Continued

The choice of wood for your cordwood building is determined by many factors:

- Where you live
- What wood grows in your area
- What wood is available
- What wood is best for cordwood
- Cost

Jack Henstridge used to advise "Use what you have at hand." This is sage advice from a master cordwood builder, but what if you have many species of wood at hand?

One of the most frequently asked "cordwood questions" is: *"What type of wood should I use?"* As a general rule of thumb nearly any type of barked, split, dry softwood is suitable for cordwood. However, there are good, better and best choices and one must approach the selection process as one would view a continuum. Soft, low density, decay resistant woods are to be preferred for their higher R-factor, light weight, easier "barkability" and for their ability to better withstand the elements. Cedar, Locust, Catalpa and Cypress fit nicely at the top end of the continuum. Tamarack, Douglas Fir, Southern and Eastern White Pine would be next, with the other Pines (red, lodge pole, yellow, etc.) and poplar, spruce, aspen and balsam not far behind. Hardwoods bring up the rear because of their tendency to swell and crack mortar joints and should be avoided if possible.

To determine "the good, the bad and the overpriced" in your area, one needs to find out what wood is available and how many "shekels" it costs per cord. With these variables in mind it would be wise to contact and question your local forestry agent, agricultural extension liaison, public library, loggers, log cabin builders, and pulp/lumber mills to resolve which timber best serves your needs without emptying your pocketbook. Needless to say, the "answer" is different in each individual case. I've used a mixture of aspen, maple, cedar and tamarack in a small, cordwood outbuilding and find the random amalgamation strikingly beautiful. If you have the time you should build a small outbuilding to determine what best suits your "eye" and your pocketbook.

  Having said all that, <u>if you can find cedar, get cedar</u>. It is the gold standard for cordwood (naturally rot resistant, light, good r-value, easy to peel, easy to lift). It will repay you in the little bit extra you spend for it.

Treating the Wood

Considerations learned from 30+ years of cordwood building

First of all it is important to know that "softwood" is the better choice for cordwood in almost all instances (as opposed to a "hardwood"). The designation softwood means trees that have needles (conifers) and a hardwood is a tree that has leaves (deciduous).

- Softwoods are, for the most part, less dense, have more air spaces (and therefore a higher R-value) and do not swell and crack mortar joints.
- Hardwoods are denser, have fewer air spaces, have a tendency to swell and crack mortar joints and move posts off their moorings.

It is important to use, if available, a softwood that can be peeled, cut to length, split (70%) and dried to its lowest moisture content (approximately 12% in most areas—see the Equilibrium Moisture Content table in this book for specific moisture contents).

The wood of choice for cordwood is "cedar." If you compare the volumetric shrinkage rate of Northern White Cedar (7.2) to Red Oak (13.7), it is easy to see why cedar is an ideal wood for cordwood. Cedar also has a pleasing fragrance, is light in weight, dries well and is naturally rot resistant.

The question could be asked, "What if I don't have cedar?" Rest easy 'Pilgrim,' there are other softwoods that can be used for cordwood construction. Red and white pine, tamarack, quaking aspen, poplar, fir and spruce have all been successfully used.

Using the hardwood that is available for a post and beam framework is an option. Personally, I find it helpful to go to the local sawyers and foresters to ascertain the drying times and specific strengths and weaknesses of each local species and then make my decision based on that information.

To Treat or Not to Treat, that is the question?

The science and lore of cordwood construction has come a long way since the early 1970's. Homes and buildings have been built of hardwood, softwood, treated with all manner of preservatives and sealers, treated with nothing and covered with stucco.

What has worked and what has not?

- Most cordwood builders have not used any treatment for their log ends.
- Some folks experimented with linseed oil, stains, paints, sealers and such and there has been no consensus on what has worked and what has not.
- Most would agree that treating with anything that would seal the log end or add a poison to the log end is not advisable.

Sandy Clidaras of Quebec, Canada has developed an effective method for treating log ends. Sandy treats log ends with safe products that preserve the log ends and maintain their natural color. (See pages 96-100 for further explanation from Sandy himself).

Most of the preservative treatments involve the use of a **borax** (borate or boron) solution on the wood, so it acts as a **preservative, an insecticide and a fungicide**. The log ends can be sprayed, dipped, or dunked.

Most log home products manufacturers have borate products, for example:

Most widely known and used are: **Timbor** (borax.com), **Pentatreat** (loghomehelp.com), **Shell-Guard** and **Armor-Guard** (permachink.com), to name a few. Do an internet search to find out more.

The basic recipe for do-it-yourselfers is to use 4 cups of 20 Mule Team Borax (the laundry detergent) and a gallon of hot water. Mix well and spray, dip or brush the logs. Some folks have added a gallon of propylene glycol to the mixture to help the borax penetrate deeper into the wood fibers. The entire mixture can be slightly heated so it becomes more soluble.

Here is Perma-Chink's explanation of *Shell Guard*. "*Shell-Guard* provides protection against insects and wood rot. This new generation of preservative combines the well-known effectiveness of borates with a glycol system that increases the penetration into the wood to enhance the action of the borate. *Shell-Guard* is colorless and odorless. The glycols used are the same type as those found in many food and skin care products. *Shell-Guard* is a concentrate that is mixed with an equal amount of water, and then applied to bare wood with a brush or as a spray. Once in the wood, it will kill those insects that eat wood such as wood boring beetles and termites. It also kills the types of fungi that are responsible for rot and decay. *Shell-Guard* makes wood toxic to wood destroying organisms. The best thing about *Shell-Guard* is that one application will last the life of your home as long as the exterior surfaces are maintained with a quality, water resistant stain such as Lifeline."

Shell Guard Concentrate in the one gallon container. In the picture it rests on large Tamarack log ends which have been treated, dried and had their primary check stuffed with white fiberglass. This was completed on the inside of a warm building so the wood was ready to use in the spring.

Drying the wood

Once you have your wood, take the bark off (use a peeling spud, a straightened garden hoe, or a sharpened car leaf spring). THEN cut the wood into your chosen length. Current cordwood theory suggests making your walls as thick as possible for extra R-value.

Barking (Debarking) Peeling Tools

4.1 The four tools shown all serve one purpose: peeling the bark off wood. From left to right they are:

- An **ice chipper/scraper** with a straight neck, used for chopping ice on sidewalks.

- A **long-handled shovel** (sharpened) is excellent for large logs with few branches. All my expert sources preach that the logs peel easiest if cut in the spring, after the sap rises.

- A **double handled draw shave** or draw knife.

- A regular **garden hoe with the neck straightened** (heat it and bend it)-this is my personal favorite because it is a bit springy and you can really get your shoulder into the bark.

The tool on the top of the pile is an old fashioned log carrier. Put the pinchers on the log and one person lifts from each side. Strong back required!

But no matter what, peeling is hard, dirty work, so "grit your teeth and get barking!"

Bucking up your Wood

Cutting your wood into lengths is another sweat-equity part of the "cordwood deal." Cordwood masons have used a variety of techniques:

- **Chain Saw**—This is the most commonly used method. Some have fastened a measuring guide to the bolts that hold the bar. Others have a "notching stick" with marks to scribe onto each log, still others have built chop saw-like tables to help with consistent log length. Logs can vary as much as ½ inch in length. Keep the inside wall as level and plumb as possible.

- **Buzz Saw**—This is my favorite way to 'buck up' cordwood. We set a 4" x 4" squared post in the ground and put the buzz saw blade the correct distance away from it (i.e. if your walls are to be 16", set the post 16" away from the blade).

Use caution and safety equipment: Goggles, gloves, chainsaw chaps, steel toed boots. This is dangerous work and you need to be alert and careful.

4.2 Bucking up wood with a buzz saw is one of the fastest ways to get it cut and drying.

Note: The vertical green metal stake was used as cut-off guide. Check your log width measurements early and often. A 16" cut off can become 17" very quickly

Chapter 5 Drying your wood (Forest Product Laboratory)

Wood Shrinkage Table: The following tables, charts and commentary are reproduced from the **Wood Handbook** (published as public domain) by the Forest Products Laboratory in Madison, Wisconsin. This USDA document FPL-GTR-113 is a wealth of information on wood, wood drying, shrinkage, moisture, finishing, etc. It is available, in its entirety, for free, online at:

http://www.fpl.fs.fed.us/documnts/fplgtr/fplgtr113/fplgtr113.htm

Some wood terms to learn:
o **Radial** Shrinkage: **Is defined as shrinkage** *across* **the annual growth rings.**
o **Tangential** Shrinkage: **Is defined as shrinkage in the** *direction of the annual growth rings.*
o **Volumetric** Shrinkage: **Is defined as shrinkage of the** *total mass* **of the wood.** If one adds the radial shrinkage + the tangential shrinkage it will closely approximate the total volumetric shrinkage.
o **Longitudinal** Shrinkage: **is defined as shrinkage** *parallel to the grain.*
Wood shrinks most in the direction of the annual growth rings (tangential), about half as much across the rings (radial), and only slightly along the grain (longitudinal).

Moisture Equilibrium Content Table:

The table on page 58 gives the recommended moisture content values for various woods at the time of installation. For example: Exterior wood, timbers and trim should be at an average of 12% moisture content when building. In the dry southwestern area of the U.S. the moisture content should be 9% and in the damp, warm costal areas, the average is 12%.

Accelerating Drying

The *Wood Handbook* suggest a method of accelerating **air drying by using fans** to force air through lumber piles "in a covered shed." The shed protects the wood from the elements and the fans improve the air circulation. <u>A **moisture meter** is a very handy device to have to check the moisture content of your wood, timbers and framing members,</u> before you build with them., thus avoiding building with lumber that is too "green." A Google search online will give you many different types and price ranges. I borrow one from my local "sawyer."

Wood Shrinkage Table   **3-5. Shrinkage values of domestic woods**

Species	Shrinkage (%) green to dry			Species	Shrinkage (%) green to dry		
	Radial	Tangential	Volumetric		Radial	Tangential	Volumetric
Hardwoods				**Oak, white--con.**			
Alder, red	4.4	7.3	12.6	Chestnut			
Ash				Live	6.6	9.5	14.7
Black	5.0	7.8	15.2	Overcup	5.3	12.7	16.0
Blue	3.9	6.5	11.7	Post	5.4	9.8	16.2
Green	4.6	7.1	12.5	Swamp, chestnut	5.2	10.8	16.4
Oregon	4.1	8.1	13.2	White	5.6	10.5	16.3
Pumpkin	3.7	6.3	12.0	Persimmon.	7.9	11.2	19.1
White	4.9	7.8	13.3	Sassafras	4.0	6.2	10.3
Aspen				Sweetgum	5.3	10.2	15.8
Bigtooth	3.3	7.9	11.8	Sycamore.	5.0	8.4	14.1
Quaking	3.5	6.7	11.5	Tanoak	4.9	11.7	17.3
Basswood.	6.6	9.3	15.8	Tupelo			
Beech.	5.5	11.9	17.2	Black	5.1	8.7	14.4
Birch				Water	4.2	7.6	12.5
Alaska paper	6.5	9.9	16.7	Walnut, black	5.5	7.8	12.8
Gray	5.2		14.7	Willow, black	3.3	8.7	13.9
Paper	6.3	8.6	16.2	Yellow-poplar	4.6	82	12.7
River	4.7	9.2	13.5	**Softwoods**			
Sweet	6.5	9.0	15.6	Cedar			
Yellow	7.3	9.5	16.8	Yellow	2.8	6.0	9.2
Buckeye,	3.6	8.1	12.5	Atlantic white	2.9	5.4	8.8
Butternut	3.4	6.4	10.6	Eastern redcedar	3.1	4.7	7.8
Cherry, black	3.7	7.1	11.5	Incense	3.3	5.2	7.7
Chestnut,	3.4	6.7	11.6	Northern white	2.2	4.9	7.2
Hardwoods—				**Softwoods-cont.**			
Cottonwood				Port-Orford	4.6	6.9	10.1
Balsam	3.0	7.1	10.5	Western redcedar	2.4	5.0	6.8
Black	3.6	8.6	12.4	Douglas-fir.			
Eastern	3.9	9.2	13.9	Coast'	4.8	7.6	12.4
Elm				Interior north'	3.8	6.9	10.7
American	4.2	9.5	14.6	Interior west[b]	4.8	7.5	11.8
Cedar	4.7	10.2	15.4	Fir			
Rock	4.8	8.1	14.9	Balsam	2.9	6.9	11.2
Slippery	4.9	8.9	13.8	California red	4.5	7.9	11.4
Winged	5.3	11.6	17.7	Grand	3.4	7.5	11.0
Hackberry	4.8	8.9	13.8	Noble	4.3	8.3	12.4
Hickory, pecan	4.9	8.9	13.6	Pacific silver	4.4	9.2	13.0
Hickory, true				Subalpine	2.6	7.4	9.4
Mockernut	7.7	11.0	17.8	White	3.3	7.0	9.8
Pignut	7.2	11.5	17.9	Hemlock			
Shagbark	7.0	10.5	16.7	Eastern	3.0	6.8	9.7
Shellbark	7.6	12.6	19.2	Mountain	4.4	7.1	11.1
Holly.	4.8	9.9	16.9	Western	4.2	7.8	12.4
Honeylocust	4.2	6.6	10.8	Larch, western	4.5	9.1	14.0
Locust, black	4.6	7.2	10.2	Pine			
Madrone.	5.6	12.4	18.1	Eastern white	2.1	6.1	8.2
Magnolia				Jack	3.7	6.6	10.3
Cucumbertree	5.2	8.8	13.6	Loblolly	4.8	7.4	12.3
Southern	5.4	6.6	12.3	Lodgepole	4.3	6.7	11.1
Sweetbay	4.7	8.3	12.9	Longleaf	5.1	7.5	12.2
Maple				Pitch	4.0	7.1	10.9
Bigleaf	3.7	7.1	11.6	Pond	5.1	7.1	11.2
Black	4.8	9.3	14.0	Ponderosa	3.9	6.2	9.7
Red	4.0	8.2	12.6	Red	3.8	7.2	11.3
Silver	3.0	7.2	12.0	Shortleaf	4.6	7.7	12.3
Striped	3.2	8.6	12.3	Slash	5.4	7.6	12.1
Sugar	4.8	9.9	14.7	Sugar	2.9	5.6	7.9
Oak, red				Virginia	4.2	7.2	11.9
Black	4.4	11.1	15.1	Western white	4.1	7.4	11.8
Laurel	4.0	9.9	19.0	Redwood			
Northern red	4.0	8.6	13.7	Old growth	2.6	4.4	6.8
Pin	4.3	9.5	14.5	Young growth	2.2	4.9	7.0
Scarlet	4.4	10.8	14.7	Spruce			
Southern red	4.7	11.3	16.1	Black	4.1	6.8	11.3
Water	4.4	9.8	16.1	Engelmann	3.8	7.1	11.0
Willow	5.0	9.6	18.9	Red	3.8	7.8	11.8
Oak, white	4.4	8.8	12.7	Sitka	4.3	7.5	11.5
Burr	5.3	10.8	16.4	Tamarack	3.7	7.4	13.6

The **Equilibrium Moisture Content in the following table will give you an idea of how dry your wood should be prior to using it, in your area of the country.**

Table 12-1. Equilibrium moisture content of wood, exposed to outdoor atmosphere, in several U.S. locations in 1997

Equilibrium moisture content (%)

State	City	Jan.	Feb.	Mar.	Apr.	May	June	July	Aug.	Sept.	Oct.	Nov.	Dec.
AK	Juneau	16.5	16.0	15.1	13.9	13.6	13.9	15.1	16.5	18.1	18.0	17.7	18.1
AL	Mobile	13.8	13.1	13.3	13.3	13.4	13.3	14.2	14.4	13.9	13.0	13.7	14.0
AZ	Flagstaff	11.8	11.4	10.8	9.3	8.8	7.5	9.7	11.1	10.3	10.1	10.8	11.8
AZ	Phoenix	9.4	8.4	7.9	6.1	5.1	4.6	6.2	6.9	6.9	7.0	8.2	9.5
AR	Little Rock	13.8	13.2	12.8	13.1	13.7	13.1	13.3	13.5	13.9	13.1	13.5	13.9
CA	Fresno	16.4	14.1	12.6	10.6	9.1	8.2	7.8	8.4	9.2	10.3	13.4	16.6
CA	Los Angeles	12.2	13.0	13.8	13.8	14.4	14.8	15.0	15.1	14.5	13.8	12.4	12.1
CO	Denver	10.7	10.5	10.2	9.6	10.2	9.6	9.4	9.6	9.5	9.5	11.0	11.0
DC	Washington	11.8	11.5	11.3	11.1	11.6	11.7	11.7	12.3	12.6	12.5	122	12.2
FL	Miami	13.5	13.1	12.8	12.3	12.7	14.0	13.7	14.1	14.5	13.5	13.9	13.4
GA	Atlanta	13.3	12.3	12.0	11.8	12.5	13.0	13.8	14.2	13.9	13.0	12.9	13.2
H I	Honolulu	13.3	12.8	11.9	11.3	10.8	10.6	10.6	10.7	10.8	11.3	12.1	12.9
I D	Boise	15.2	13.5	11.1	10.0	9.7	9.0	7.3	7.3	8.4	10.0	13.3	15.2
IL	Chicago	14.2	13.7	13.4	12.5	122	12.4	12.8	13.3	13.3	12.9	14.0	14.9
IN	Indianapolis	15.1	14.6	13.8	12.8	13.0	12.8	13.9	14.5	14.2	13.7	14.8	15.7
IA	Des Moines	14.0	13.9	13.3	12.6	12.4	12.6	13.1	13.4	13.7	12.7	13.9	14.9
KS	Wichita	13.8	13.4	12.4	12.4	13.2	12.5	11.5	11.8	12.6	12.4	13.2	13.9
KY	Louisville	13.7	13.3	12.6	12.0	12.8	13.0	13.3	13.7	14.1	13.3	13.5	13.9
LA	New Orleans	14.9	14.3	14.0	14.2	14.1	14.6	15.2	15.3	14.8	14.0	14.2	15.0
ME	Portland	13.1	12.7	12.7	12.1	12.6	13.0	13.0	13.4	13.9	13.8	14.0	13.5
MA	Boston	11.8	11.6	11.9	11.7	12.2	12.1	11.9	12.5	13.1	12.8	12.6	12.2
MI	Detroit	14.7	14.1	13.5	12.6	12.3	12.3	12.6	13.3	13.7	13.5	14.4	15.1
MN	Minneapolis-St.Paul	13.7	13.6	13.3	12.0	11.9	12.3	12.5	13.2	13.8	13.3	14.3	14.6
MS	Jackson	15.1	14.4	13.7	13.8	14.1	13.9	14.6	14.6	14.6	14.1	14.3	14.9
MO	St. Louis	14.5	14.1	13.2	12.4	12.8	12.6	12.9	13.3	13.7	13.1	14.0	14.9
MT	Missoula	16.7	15.1	12.8	11.4	11.6	11.7	10.1	9.8	11.3	12.9	16.2	17.6
NE	Omaha	14.0	13.8	13.0	12.1	12.6	12.9	13.3	13.8	14.0	13.0	13.9	14.8
NV	Las Vegas	8.5	7.7	7.0	5.5	5.0	4.0	4.5	52	5.3	5.9	7.2	8.4
NV	Reno	12.3	10.7	9.7	8.8	8.8	8.2	7.7	7.9	8.4	9.4	10.9	12.3
NM	Albuquerque	10.4	9.3	8.0	6.9	6.8	6.4	8.0	8.9	8.7	8.6	9.6	10.7
N Y	New York	12.2	11.9	11.5	11.0	11.5	11.8	11.8	12.4	12.6	12.3	12.5	12.3
NC	Raleigh	12.8	12.1	12.2	11.7	13.1	13.4	13.8	14.5	14.5	13.7	12.9	12.8
ND	Fargo	14.2	14.6	15.2	12.9	11.9	12.9	13.2	13.2	13.7	13.5	15.2	15.2
OH	Cleveland	14.6	14.2	13.7	12.6	12.7	12.7	12.8	13.7	13.8	13.3	13.8	14.6
OK	Oklahoma City	13.2	12.9	122	12.1	13.4	13.1	11.7	11.8	12.9	12.3	12.8	13.2
OR	Pendleton	15.8	14.0	11.6	10.6	9.9	9.1	7.4	7.7	8.8	11.0	14.6	16.5
OR	Portland	16.5	15.3	14.2	13.5	13.1	12.4	11.7	11.9	12.6	15.0	16.8	17.4
PA	Philadelphia	12.6	11.9	11.7	11.2	11.8	11.9	12.1	12.4	13.0	13.0	12.7	12.7
SC	Charleston	13.3	12.6	12.5	12.4	12.8	13.5	14.1	14.6	14.5	13.7	13.2	13.2
SD	Sioux Falls	14.2	14.6	142	12.9	12.6	12.8	12.6	13.3	13.6	13.0	14.6	15.3
TN	Memphis	13.8	13.1	12.4	12.2	12.7	12.8	13.0	13.1	13.2	12.5	12.9	13.6
1X	Dallas-Ft.Worth	13.6	13.1	12.9	13.2	13.9	13.0	11.6	11.7	12.9	12.8	13.1	13.5
TX	El Paso	9.6	8.2	7.0	5.8	6.1	6.3	8.3	9.1	9.3	8.8	9.0	9.8
UT	Salt Lake City	14.6	13.2	11.1	10.0	9.4	8.2	7.1	7.4	8.5	10.3	12.8	14.9
VA	Richmond	13.2	12.5	12.0	11.3	12.1	12.4	13.0	13.7	13.8	13.5	12.8	13.0
WA	Seattle-Tacoma	15.6	14,6	15.4	13.7	13.0	12.7	12.2	12.5	13.5	15.3	16.3	16.5
W I	Madison	14.5	14.3	14.1	12.8	12.5	12.8	13.4	14.4	14.9	14.1	15.2	15.7
WV	Charleston	13.7	13.0	12.1	11.4	12.5	13.3	14.1	14.3	14.0	13.6	13.0	13.5
W Y	Cheyenne	10.2	10.4	10.7	10.4	10.8	10.5	9.9	9.9	9.7	9.7	10.6	10.6

'EMC values were determined from the average of 30 or more years of relative humidity and temperature data available from the National Climatic Data Center of the National Oceanic and Atmospheric Administration.

61

The three "Must Do" rules for wood preparation:

1. Bark it.
2. Split it. (70%)
3. Dry it.

Drying the Wood

Round logs will need at least 12 to 18 months to dry, if covered in a single row. If you split the wood in halves and quarters the drying time can be reduced.

4.3 Drying a single, long "rick" of wood, in the sun, with the top covered, is the most effective way to dry cordwood. (Novitch).

When the wood is very dry, "popcorn dry," you should be able to take two logs in hand and smack them together so they make a hollow "popping" sound. You could also get a moisture meter from the local lumber yard to check the exact moisture content. It is important to get the wood as dry as possible for your region. Refer to the Equilibrium Moisture Content tables (page 60) to see how dry your wood should be.

Split vs. Round
The wood can be left round, all split or just a percentage split. All three techniques work, but the split wood dries faster and doesn't loosen in the wall as easily as full rounds.

4.4 An excellent example of cordwood walls with 70% split and 30% round within a post and beam frame- work. The split logs dry faster, don't crack as much and look very nice with the rounds.

Dry the Wood: My narrative on log loosening and splitting log ends

When I built my cordwood home in 1979 I used Northern White Cedar from the swamps of Northern Wisconsin that had been winter-cut four years earlier. It had been stacked, off the ground, with the bark on. I peeled and cut the logs.

The logs then seasoned for 12 months and construction began. My walls are 90% round and 10% split. A year after my home was up approximately 20% of the logs had loosened and some of the larger rounds had developed a large check that went all the way through to the outside (a rather drafty problem in -20 below weather). I stuffed these checks with white fiberglass and caulked around the loosened logs with Perma-Chink (Log Jam). Needless to say I wondered about a permanent solution to this (pardon my pun) "Post Erection, Log Loosening Headache." As luck would have it, I then built four cordwood pole sheds at cordwood workshops held in the mid-80's. On each of these buildings we experimented with different types of wood. I also split ALL the wood to see if splitting would help with the log loosening problem. Well, lo and behold, IT DID. The split logs did not shrink or develop the large checks that round logs did. Another advantage to split wood is that it dries quicker. You can see the small little cracks develop on the end of the logs as they dry (anyone who has cut and dried firewood understands this process). You can also purchase or borrow a moisture meter (small saw mill owners sometimes have these) to get to the proper moisture content for dry wood for your climate.

So I began suggesting to split approximately 70% of their wood and if they wanted to use large round pieces to dry them inside, by the wood stove (or a heat source) and then fill the checks with caulk or fiberglass (or both). There are now seven cordwood homes built near my little piece of heaven that are built with 70% or more split wood. Guess what, they have much less log-loosening.

It is important to remember that some logs will loosen no matter how careful you are and one of the realities of cordwood is that those logs that loosen will have to be dealt with in one of the manners suggested. Some unfortunate cordwood builders who have used undried, unsplit cordwood have had EVERY log loosen!

Remember, it is wise to read all you can and then build a practice building. Talk with people who have built cordwood. Dave Barry once said, "It was amateurs that built the Ark and professionals who built the Titanic." An informed amateur with patience and foresight and a discerning mind, CAN build his/her own home.

How many full cords (4' x 4' x 8') of wood do you need?

The Formulas
To determine the approximate <u>number of cords of wood needed</u>, calculate the number of square feet of interior wall and multiply by .015 for a 24" wall, .01 for a 16" wall and .0075 for a 12" wall. :

> Number of sq. ft. of interior wall surface area x .015 = full cords of wood required for a 24" wall. Use .01 for a 16" wall and .0075 for a 12" wall. (Courtesy of the U. of Manitoba)

For example: building size 30'x 40'= 30 + 40 + 30 + 40 = 140 ft. x 8' = 1120 sq. ft. of interior wall surface area. Multiply 1120 x .01 (for a 16" wall) and you'll need 11.2 full cords (4' x 4' x 8') of wood.

For example:

Square Feet	Wall Thickness	Number of Full Cords of Wood
1,200	16 inches	12
1,200	24 inches	18

Add an extra cord of wood to be safe. This calculation assumes 20% of wall space will be doors & windows. Formulas are courtesy of Dr. Kris Dick, P.Eng.

> ### Another method: Using Face Cords or Single Cords
>
> A "face cord" or "single cord" is a stack of wood 4' high, 8' wide and 16 inches deep. (This equals 32 sq. ft.) 32 sq. ft. becomes the number to use when figuring how much wood is needed.
>
> One can usually "get" 2.5 face cords from a "full cord." A builder can use face cords to determine the amount of wood needed to build.   Just like for the University of Manitoba's formula above, figure the number of square feet of interior wall space.   Then subtract the square footage of window and door space.   Then subtract 20% of that total for mortar joints. Divide this by 32 sq. ft. and this will be the number of face cords needed to build.
>
> For example: building size 30'x 40'= 30 + 40 + 30 + 40 = 140 ft. x 8' = 1120 sq. ft. of interior wall surface area.   Subtract the sq. ft. amount of window and door space (200 sq. ft.) 1120- 200 = 920 sq. ft. Multiply by 20% for mortar joints 920 x .20 = 184. Then subtract 184 from 920; 920-184= 736 sq. ft. Divide that by 32 sq. ft.= 23 face cords. Divide that by 2.5 (the number of face cords in a full cord) and it comes out to **11.5 full cords or 23 face cords.** Same number as from the University of Manitoba full cord estimate. The face cord estimate is simply a different method of arriving at the same number.

> ### *The present literature on cordwood advises a 16"-24" wall for optimum performance in the northern climes.*

R-Factor

Researchers at the University of Manitoba engineering department performed R-value testing on cordwood walls in their research facility in 2005. (The complete test results are compiled in the very handy book *Cordwood & the Code: A Building Permit Guide*). They determined that the R-value per inch of a cordwood wall (mortar, wood, insulation) was **1.47**. This means that an average, well-built cordwood home with proper mortaring techniques and dry wood will have the following R-values:

12" wall	**R 17.6**
16" wall	**R 23.5**
24" wall	**R 35.2**

Sawdust
The R-values stated above are from cordwood walls built using sawdust and lime.

Sawdust is used for the **mortar mix** and for the **insulation** in typical cordwood buildings. **The type** of sawdust obtained is very important. Do NOT use sawdust from a table saw. It is too fine. Use sawdust from a cut off saw, a buzz saw or a chain saw.
Bottom line: The sawdust needs to be **coarse.**

The Sawdust is for two tasks:

You need two different piles of sawdust (put tarps over the piles):

- **Dry sawdust mixed with lime for insulation.**

- **Soaked sawdust for the mortar mix.**

1. **Sawdust for mortar:** This needs to be coarse. Cured, softwood sawdust is the best. Do not use hardwood sawdust, it will not hold as much water, because it is so dense. It needs to be soaked for 24 hours before using in a mortar mix. The main function of the soaked sawdust is to slow the set & cure of the mortar by slowing releasing moisture into the mortar bed in your wall.

2.   **Sawdust for insulation:** This is also best if it is coarse, softwood sawdust. Mix it with hydrated lime (9:1 ratio) so that every piece of sawdust has some lime sticking to it. The lime is used as an insect repellant. This is then packed and tamped into the central cavity as you build each wall section.

NEW additions/substitutions for <u>sawdust</u> to the traditional portland and lime based cordwood mortar mix:

We have been experimenting with different types of substitutes for sawdust in the mortar mix and for insulation.

Here are three we have used:

1. **Cellulose**--This is the type of insulation sold in building supply stores. It is for blowing into the wall cavity or ceiling. Usually it has been treated with borax or a borate solution and some has been treated with ammonium sulfate (as fire retardants). This is basically recycled, treated newspaper. It works well in the mortar mix and in the insulation cavity.

2. **Hemp Hurds**--These are the waste product from industrial hemp. It is illegal to grow industrial hemp in the US. We used this product at the Cordwood Conference at the University of Manitoba in Winnipeg, Canada where growing industrial hemp is legal. These hurds are little sections of stalks that are about ½" to 1" long. They soak up moisture like crazy and are very useful in creating a mix that slows the set and cure of the mortar by releasing moisture as the mortar dries. We also used hemp hurds mixed with lime as insulation in the center cavity.

3. **Sharp Gravel**--½" small, sharp gravel.   This is like pea gravel, but the sharp kind. Jack Henstridge suggested this be used to add strength and mass to the cordwood mortar. Sandy Clidaras of Quebec has used this in his traditional cordwood mortar mix with good success. The amount used is a ½ shovelful per full mix. The gravel may affect the tuck pointing and final finishing of the wall, so the amount to add is still under experimentation.   You will have to be the final judge of how smooth you want your mortar, if you choose to use gravel.

Chapter 6   Mortar Mixes

1. **Traditional Cordwood Mortar**
2. **Lime Putty Mortar (LPM)**
3. **Paper Enhanced Mortar (PEM)**
4. **Cellulose Enhanced Mortar (CEM)**
5. **Cob Mortar**

1. Traditional Cordwood Lime & Portland Mortars

Perhaps the most critical phase of cordwood construction is in the choice of a thick, slow-drying, slow-curing, workable mortar mix. There is one basic consideration: Is the cordwood wall to be load bearing (curved wall, round, stackwall) or not (post and beam.) If the wall is to be load bearing, the mixture needs to be stronger (i.e. more portland) than if using a post and beam framework to hold the roof. The use of sawdust with the basic sand, cement and lime (or masonry cement) is an innovation that has been very successful. The sawdust slows down the "set" of the mortar, thereby reducing mortar cracking. It gives the mortar an "adobe-clay" feel and is quite thick and malleable. After a little experimentation the following mix was developed.

My Favorite Mix: for a non-load bearing wall

3 parts sand
2+ parts sawdust (soaked overnight)
1 part Portland cement
1 part Type S hydrated lime

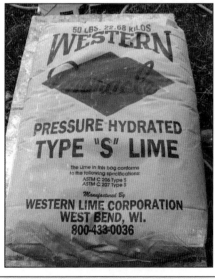

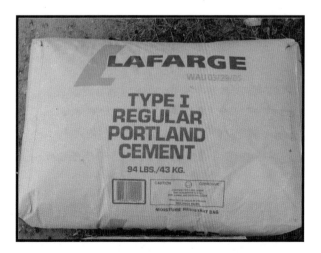

Type S Masons Hydrated Lime   *Type 1 Portland Cement*

If you choose a load-bearing wall (no post & beam framework), cut the sawdust to one shovelful/part. The question could logically be asked, "Can one use masonry cement rather than Portland cement?" And the answer is, "Of course!" Masonry cement is nothing more than Portland cement mixed with crushed lime (not hydrated lime which helps to "heal over" mortar cracks). Here are two additional mixes.

Masonry cement mix:

3 parts sand
2 parts sawdust—1 part sawdust if load-bearing
1-1/2 parts masonry cement
1 part hydrated lime

Rob Roy's mix:

9 parts sand
3 parts soaked sawdust (overnight)
3 parts hydrated lime
2 parts Portland cement

6.1 Write the __mix__ you choose on a board with permanent marker. This helps to eliminates mistakes. Trust me on this one.

Some people like to soak their sawdust overnight in a 55 gallon drum (I like to use a "kiddie" swimming pool). Some also advocate using a 3-1-1 mixing ratio when shoveling the batch into the wheelbarrow or cement mixer. The lime brightens up the wall and makes for a lighter room. When paneling first came into widespread use, many people bought very dark, walnut-shaded paneling and the rooms looked small and "cavey." Now there is an incredible amount of light-colored paneling being used and the rooms look light and open. So, to lighten the cordwood wall (which is 60% or more log ends) put a little extra lime in the mortar, which will enhance the feeling of space and increase light reflection in the room.

Over the years I have found that using a CEMENT MIXER or better yet a MORTAR MIXER is the best way to save one's back and energy for mortaring.

6.2 This is a good layout for mixing mortar. A cement mixer (a mortar mixer is even better) soaked sawdust to the right, sand right behind, Portland cement & hydrated lime to the left. Keep your workstation clean, well managed and the job will go much smoother. (R. Flatau)

SPEED TIP: To get more done in less time! When working alone I would mix a batch of mortar, and take it to the wall section where I was working. I would go back to the mixer and dry mix the next batch. When just about finished mortaring, I would add water to the dry mix. This kept me with a fresh batch of mortar in a timely fashion. This technique was best done while working on the lower stages of the wall—which go up the quickest. NOTE: You cannot leave a batch of mortar in the machine indefinitely; 15-30 minutes (with the mixer running) is the max. NOTE: As the wall rises, the last three feet take as much time as the first five feet.

Use Safety Gear when mixing mortar: a dust mask, safety glasses and a good pair of masonry gloves will make your experience safer.

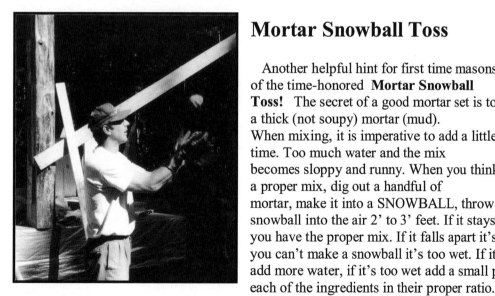

Mortar Snowball Toss

Another helpful hint for first time masons is the use of the time-honored **Mortar Snowball Toss!** The secret of a good mortar set is to start with a thick (not soupy) mortar (mud).
When mixing, it is imperative to add a little water at a time. Too much water and the mix becomes sloppy and runny. When you think you have a proper mix, dig out a handful of mortar, make it into a SNOWBALL, throw the snowball into the air 2' to 3' feet. If it stays in shape, you have the proper mix. If it falls apart it's too dry, if you can't make a snowball it's too wet. If it's too dry add more water, if it's too wet add a small portion of each of the ingredients in their proper ratio.
Experiment with your mixture before you build. Add an extra half-shovelful of lime or half shovelful of cement if you want the wall a bit stronger and lighter, but don't overdo it or it will crack and shrink around the logs. Change the mix as it suits you and your climate.

2. LPM: Lime Putty Mortar

Rob Roy & Bruce Kilgore

Rob Roy & Bruce Kilgore have been experimenting with lime putty mortar in an effort to use a mortar that doesn't use Portland cement and the inherent "embodied energy" that is used in the production of Portland cement.

They used the traditional Type S hydrated builder's lime. After mixing the lime with water and letting it sit (hydrate) for five days, they mixed the pure lime mortar with sand (2.5 sand, 1 lime mortar) to create a workable lime mortar mud. The mortar pointed well and looks, for all intents and purposes, like a traditional cordwood wall made with Portland, hydrated lime, sand and sawdust. The pure lime mortar is very light in color and has a good track record (this is what the Romans used 2000 years ago). Here is a condensed update from Rob & Bruce which appeared in the *Cordwood Conference Papers 2011*.

Making lime putty LPM and keeping it

"Over the past five years, we have seen that success with LPM is a matter of minimizing variables. Careful quality control has produced good results, whereas there have been failures where variables are not kept within best practices.

Making the Lime Putty Mortar	The Mortar Mix
4.5 gallons water to (1) 50# bag of Lime	1 part Lime Putty Mortar 2.5 parts washed, mason's sand

Get the right Lime The first and most important variable is to use the right lime, which is dry hydrated "type S" lime, which comes in 50-pound bags. Bruce Kilgore is a stickler for getting his lime as fresh as possible. He has noted varying bag weights, by 5 pounds and more, and it is expected that this discrepancy may indicate more or less moisture in the product.

Accuracy in measure … is important, for making lime putty. Kilgore weighs three bags of lime in pounds. Then he measures out a weight of water which is three-quarters the weight of the lime. If three bags weigh 160 pounds, for example, he mixes in 120 pounds of water to make the lime putty. He starts with about a third of the water in the bottom of a plastic vessel made from half of a 55-gallon plastic drum. He adds a bag of lime and lets it percolate in and homogenizes it with a paddle mixer attached to a strong (1/2 HP) electric drill. Then he adds another third of the measured water, another bag of lime, and repeats the procedure, and then once more. The lime putty is allowed to hydrate five days.

Roy's method is based on water volume. He does not weigh the bags, but is also careful to obtain fresh lime of the right kind in unbroken 50-pound bags. Roy distributes 2.25 gallons of water in each of two plastic 5-gallon pails, and then splits a 50-pound bag of lime between the two pails. He lets the lime percolate into the water, then mixes it with a paddle mixer.

By either method, cover the vessel with plastic. The lime putty is ready to use after five days, but will only get better with age. Kilgore has used it after weeks, even months, with excellent results. With either method: wear a respiration mask when dumping the bags of lime putty. The dust is nasty and caustic.

Sand, a critical variable. Both authors use the same fine masonry sand used with Portland-based cordwood mortar. Theoretically, a coarser sand should work, but using coarse sand at a Colorado workshop resulted in a less cohesive (plastic) mortar to work with, and, ultimately, the mortar became crumbly, which may have had more to do with the extreme drying conditions in the clear dry air at 8200 feet. Roy's son, conducted another workshop in similar conditions, with similar results: weak, crumbly mortar.

Of great importance is that the sand be kept dry. If it is too wet, it will not be possible to mix a stiff enough mix to use with cordwood masonry. So get dry sand, and *keep it dry* by keeping it well-covered. You can add water to a mix, if needed, but you can't take it out if the mortar is too wet before any water is added. Both authors rarely have had to add water to the mix, although they have both done so with very dry sand. You cannot add dry lime to the mix in order to stiffen it. All lime used must hydrate a minimum of five days.

Mixing the LPM. Author Kilgore, a stickler for detail and consistency, measures each wheelbarrow load (batch) by weight: 75 pounds of sand and 28 pounds of lime putty, already prepared as described above. He mixes the ingredients first with a hoe until the mix is of a consistent color throughout. Then he "kneads" the mortar with his gloved hands against one end of the barrel, much as pizza dough is kneaded. He kneads the mortar towards one end of the wheelbarrow, then the other. If it passes the stiffness tests (see below), it is finished.

Rob works with volume, not weight, beginning with a level 5-gallon pail of sand and a level two-gallon container of lime putty. He places about half of the sand in a wheelbarrow, adds all of the lime putty, and mixes it thoroughly with a garden hoe until it has the consistency - and appearance - of marshmallow fluff. To this he adds the remaining sand and works it over until the mix has a consistent texture. Influenced by Kilgore's success, Roy has also adopted the kneading technique, which drives the lime into the sand voids much more effectively then simply turning and chopping with a hoe.

Organizing the mixing area. Author Kilgore takes great care to organize his mixing area for efficiency and consistency of mixing. He uses six lime putty drums, each one being a half of a 55-gallon plastic drum, ripped along its waist with a circular saw. He labels each batch with its date of mixture, so that he is always using lime putty at least 3 days old, and preferably 5 or more. (Once, when 2-day old lime putty was accidentally used in the mix, cracks formed in the masonry a few days later.) Plastic covers the half-barrels and the entire site is under cover.

Kilgore's sand is dry and under a tarp and he brings a quantity of it to the mixing area as needed. He has scales for weighing water, sand, and lime putty and uses them with every batch.

Testing and consistency. Both authors test the mortar for consistency. A snowball sized ball of mortar caught from a three-foot high toss should neither shatter nor collapse in a soft "sploot," like the product from the business end of a cow. It should be cohesive and plastic, and rather more stiff than brick or block mortar. We are looking for what is known as "stone mortar." It should support itself along the steep side of the wheelbarrow without slumping. Mortar which is too wet is sticky and difficult to work with and is more prone to shrinkage cracking as all that water is transpired out during drying. Mortar too dry is harder to place as it is less plastic. More will spill onto the ground. If the mortar is too dry,

Wear safety gear when making LPM.

a little water can be added and the batch mixed again. If the mix is too wet, a little dry sand may be added, but not dry lime.

Using lime putty mortar with cordwood masonry. Work in the shade, whenever possible. It is worth creating shade by stretching a tarp out from the roofed timber frame. (The advantages of building cordwood masonry under the umbrella protection of a roofed timber frame are well-known: it makes the building inspector happy, and the masonry work takes place out of the rain and direct sun.)

In normal drying conditions, we rough-point the wall as we build, leaving about a quarter inch of the log-ends "proud" of the mortar background. Normally, final or "finished" pointing is done by the end of the workday, although one couple of our acquaintance was very happy with the husband building the cordwood wall one day and his wife coming along the next morning and pointing it. LPM might take two weeks to get fully hard and strong, but we have not been limited as to how high a wall we could build in a day. The labor-intensive nature of cordwood masonry comes into play - how much you can actually do in a day - long before the mortar's initial load-bearing strength. LPM is much faster and easier than pointing cement-based mortars. It is more plastic and smoother.

Pay attention to detail. Lime putty mortar is not for everyone. Success with LPM - and there have been failures - depends upon minimizing variables, as described above. If you are not a detail person, use a more forgiving Portland recipe.

The authors cannot emphasize strongly enough the advantage of doing a test project with LPM before purchasing large amounts of lime and embarking on a 1500 SF house. The test project can be a little garden shed, or a back panel of the house which might be hidden in some way. At the least, try several batches in a test frame and wait a couple of weeks to see how it performs. If successful, keep up the same methodology. If unsuccessful, try something different. Experiment further with the LPM … or switch to Portland cordwood mortar mix.

This article is condensed from Rob & Bruce's article in the Cordwood Conference Papers 2011. It is used with permission.

6.3 Nerdwood, the double wall, LPM home of Greg and Clare in the Upper Peninsula of Michigan is a beautiful work in progress.
www.nerdwood.com

Contact Information:
Rob Roy, Earthwood Building School
366 Murtagh Hill Road, West Chazy, NY 12992
robandjaki@yahoo.com   www.cordwoodmasonry.com
518-493-7744

3. PEM: Paper Enhanced Mortar

Alan Stankevitz

It's been years since the *2005 Continental Cordwood Conference Papers* were published. In the papers, I wrote an article about PEM titled, "What's Black and White and Mortared All Over?" The paper focused on its evolution from what is commonly known as "papercrete" and gave the necessary steps to make PEM—**P**aper **E**nhanced **M**ortar. In this paper I will focus on the durability and the benefits of using this mortar for cordwood wall construction.

A Bit of Background

Our house is 2-stories, 16-sided, post and beam frame with double walls constructed of cordwood. This means there are a total of 32 exterior and 32 interior cordwood walls that are approximately 8'x8' in dimension. 64 cordwood walls may seem like a daunting task (and it is) but we (my wife Jo and I) wanted an energy efficient home that would keep us cozy through adverse weather conditions. Our house is nearly

air-tight and has plenty of insulation and thermal mass in our walls. Typically we only need to add supplemental heating to the house during the heart of the winter; otherwise our house is entirely heated by active and passive solar heating systems.

Prior to the construction of our house, Rob Roy mentioned a house being built near him by James Juczak. Jim was experimenting with using papercrete as a mortar. It wasn't very long before I was on the phone with Jim discussing the merits of using papercrete as a mortar. In Jim's case, he was fortunate to have a nearby source of paper sludge—the byproduct of a paper mill. Jim didn't have to slurry his paper, it was already slurried for him.

In my particular case, I had to make the slurry myself out of recycled newspapers with the shiny ads removed. This made for a little more work, but I could control the quality of the paper being used with the mix.

Our first cordwood wall was constructed in May of 2001 and it was made out of papercrete. Papercrete is nothing more than a combination of portland cement and paper. Typically, homes built from papercrete are built from cured blocks of the material, stacked like bricks.

In Jim's case, he was simply mixing up the sludge and masonry cement and using it as mortar. I did the same and the results were mixed (no pun intended). It was quite plyable, but it had loads of water in it.

(To backtrack just for a paragraph here, I had done a test wall with papercrete prior to using it on our house. The test wall came out just fine, but it was built without a post and beam frame and it was smaller than our 8' x 8' walls. In hindsight, I should have built it within a post and beam frame.)

Our first wall was built on the north side of the house and that in combination with the very wet mortar made me think that the wall was never, ever going to dry! Fast forwarding to six weeks later, it finally dried to a point close to its present form. Unfortunately, the whole wall shrunk. The 8' x 8' wall had a ½" gap at the top and about a ¼" gap on both sides. Hmmm…not good. No wonder why they build papercrete houses with dried blocks of the stuff. It shrinks! Lesson learned.

So now that I knew that papercrete would shrink, how was I to remedy this problem? Sand came to the rescue. Not only did the sand prevent shrinkage, the mortar was really easy to work with. And that is how PEM (Paper Enhanced Mortar) came into being. The reason I gave it this name was to differentiate it from papercrete. It is not the same. The mix I have been using has sand and more portland cement than papercrete.

10 Years After

It's been 10 years now since we started construction on the exterior cordwood walls of our house. During those 10 years, the walls have gotten a pretty good beating from wind, rain and sun even with our hefty 3-foot overhangs on both floors. Doing due diligence for this paper, I took a stroll around both floors of our house and carefully looked at each and every external wall. My goal was to find any signs of degradation of the mortar.

Looking at the walls the only sign of any degradation that I could find were a few pits in the mortar where chunks of paper once existed. My guess is that I must have been in a hurry to make slurry and the paper was not totally broken down into very fine pieces. This in

6.4 Here's a good example of how the mortar looks after 10 years. After the mortar was tuck-pointed with a bread knife, a small foam brush was used to finish off the mortar.

itself was only half of the problem because the small paper chunks would have stayed in place if it not were for my dear friends…the woodpeckers! (I have an agreement with our local woodpeckers: I keep them in suet and they keep me from yelling at them to stay off the house!) These pits are only on a few walls and are very small and not deep. You would have to look hard to find them. Besides degradation, there are the occasional shrinkage cracks – not nearly as many as I experienced with sawdust-based mortar. They are very minor and of no concern.

I realize that 10 years is not 100 years, but I do not see any reason why PEM cannot last 100 years or more based on the condition of our exterior walls as they are today. I do want to stress however that our house is supported by the walls and a post and beam frame. PEM does not have the same compression strength as regular mortar and to have it bear the entire house-load is still in question. Until some rich kid comes along and can afford to have the wall tested for compression, the verdict is still out on compression strength of PEM.

The benefits of PEM

Over the past 10 years of working with PEM and listening to others that have used it, there are many benefits to using PEM. Here's my list of reasons why you should consider using PEM for your next cordwood building project.

- **Workability** – The mortar is sticky and firm —easy to work into nooks and crannies.
- **Forgiving** – You can add too much water just as with other mixes, but it is not as critical.
- **Better R-Value** – PEM is 40% paper. This enhances the insulation value of the mortar, increasing the energy efficiency of the wall unit.

- **Environmentally Friendly** – Using waste paper for building is good for the environment.
- **Pointability** – PEM is a pleasure to point. Not only is it easy to manipulate with a finishing tool, it stays pliable much longer than regular mortar.
- **Adhesion** – The paper fibers in the mortar more readily attach themselves to the cordwood, making for a better bond with the wood.
- **Light Color** – Once PEM dries, it is quite light in color. This helps brighten up a cordwood wall which tends to suck up light.
- **Plaster** – PEM can also be used as plaster. Works great for Adobe-style walls.
- **Doesn't Need to be Babied** – I have never had to tarp a wall to keep it from drying out prematurely during hot, sunny days.
- **Very Few Shrinkage Cracks** – Yes there are some shrinkage cracks in our walls, but not nearly as many as I had with traditional cordwood mixes.

Revisions to the Mix

Since my last paper, I really haven't found any meaningful difference by adding hydrated lime to the mix and I like to keep things simple. Masonry cement already has a lime component in it.

Here's the simplified mix by volume:

6 parts drained, slurried paper
6 parts fine sand
3 parts type N masonry cement

I have been asked to provide the mix by weight, but due to the variability of the weight of water in the slurried paper, I do not recommend this. Volume seems to work best for measuring. For the actual steps involved in making PEM, please see my paper in the 2005 CoCoCo papers or visit my website: www.daycreek.com.

Excerpted from the Cordwood Conference Papers 2011 with permission.

6.5 Alan & Jo in front of an outside double wall at their cordwood castle in Minnesota. (R. Flatau)

Contact Information:
stankevitz@daycreek.com
www.daycreek.com
Alan Stankevitz
8824 County 21
La Crescent, MN 55947

4. CEM: Cellulose Enhanced Mortar

Tom Huber

CEM Update .

"For the cabin project at Cedar Eden (Potsdam, NY) I changed the mortar mix in a couple of ways. One, I used only cellulose as the insulating ingredient in the mortar versus newsprint or shredded office paper. (Both sawdust and cellulose were used to insulate between the inner

and outer mortar sections.) The 2010 chicken coop project *("Cordwood Masonry - It's For the Birds!")* demonstrated the performance superiority of using cellulose. Secondly, I incorporated hydrated lime into the mix as well, which resulted in the following mix:

> **2 parts cellulose**
> **2 parts mason's sand**
> **1 part masonry cement (Type N or S)**
> **½ part hydrated lime**

This mix worked very well. A very tight <u>friction bond with the log-ends resulted in no log loosening</u> whatsoever. The benefits of a hydrated lime – cement mortar include increased tensile bond strength due to the high water retention and low air content of the lime as well as autogenous healing (lime reacts with atmospheric carbon dioxide to knit together any future hairline cracking). <u>This very plastic, sticky mortar helps increase adherence to log-ends.</u> In addition, one could see how the increased water content in the mix was absorbed by the log-end with the closing of the end grain checks and the log-end being "locked" into the mortar matrix. The mortar dries slowly and gradually (see A. Stankevitz, et al writing on this subject), which aides in preventing cracking. Thus far, no cracking in the mortar of either CEM project has occurred. The mortar dries a nice shade of light-reflecting white. The mix is generally wetter due to the absorbing quality of the cellulose, and slight color differences resulted with different moisture content of the batches of mortar. Essentially, the wetter the mix, the whiter the color. The only drawback is that some of the log-ends develop water stains. I used a high RPM grinder to quickly sand the water stains after the wall completely cured. No resulting loosening of the log-ends (from the vibrations from the angle grinder) was observed.

I wanted this mix to be durable, insulative, and light in color while also having good thermal mass qualities for the passive solar aspect of the cabin. In retrospect, the mix was plenty dense and could probably be improved by reducing the proportion of sand. I have the back wall to complete in the cabin in the summer of 2012 and plan to make this slight adjustment to the mix resulting in the following:

2 parts cellulose
1½ part mason's sand
1 part masonry cement (Type N or S)
½ part hydrated lime (may-be eliminated)

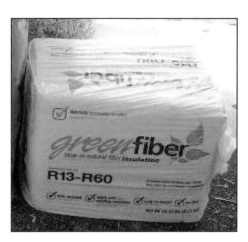

(Right) Cellulose (one type) as it comes from the building supply store.

Lastly, since most masonry cement already includes a significant portion of lime, the mix could be further simplified <u>by eliminating the hydrated lime</u> (as was suggested by Alan Stankevitz in a private communication)."

6.6 Tom Huber's Cordwood Cabin in Potsdam, NY.

Contact Information: Tom Huber
thuber@paulsmiths.edu
(518) 327-6330 (daytime)
Address: P.O. Box 58, Rainbow Lake, NY 12976

5.	Cobwood	Cordwood & Cob

There is so much interest in building with cob, that it only seems natural that people would want to combine the two techniques and replace the mortar in a cordwood wall with cob. For those readers who are unfamiliar with cob, it is a mud like concoction made up of clay, sand, straw and water. There are many different cob mixes made with varying proportions of soil, straw, amendments and water. A Google search brings numerous sites and suggestions. There have been a few cordwood and cob buildings erected. Ianto Evans has helped people build with cob and cordwood. Ianto is one of the leading experts in the "Cob field." His website is www.cobcottage.com Here is a paragraph from the website:

"Earth is probably still the world's commonest building material. The word cob comes from an old English root meaning a lump or rounded mass. Cob building uses hands and feet to form lumps of earth mixed with sand and straw, a sensory and aesthetic experience similar to sculpting with clay. Cob is easy to learn and inexpensive to build. Because there are no forms, ramming, cement or rectilinear bricks, cob lends itself to organic shapes: curved walls, arches and niches. Earth homes are cool in summer, warm in winter. Cob's resistance to rain and cold makes it ideally suited to cold climates like the Pacific Northwest, and to desert conditions."

The term *cob* is used to describe a monolithic building system based on a mixture of clay, sand and straw. The construction uses no forms, bricks or wooden framework; it is built from the ground up. To be sure, there are as many different cob mixtures as there are cob structures. Do your homework and find a mix that works for you. Here is simply one mix.

Cob Mix
Soil Containing
-30% Clay & 70%
Sand
-Straw (not hay)
-Water
www.squidoo.com

6.7 The Kinsale Theater in Ireland is made of cobwood.

The Kinsale Theater was part of a community effort to build a theater that would also have a positive impact on the group of students enrolled. The building was designed and built by the theatre students and their instructors. The cob and cordwood walls are impressive and functional. Their story first appeared in Permaculture Magazine, Issue number 45. To read a full description of the adventure online:

http://www.daycreek.com/dc/html/perma_No45.htm

Cob has also been used effectively on quite a few homes and cabins throughout the world. Tony Wrench has been a leader in cobwood building throughout Europe.

6.8 The Roundhouse is a cobwood building Tony helped erect at a workshop in Denmark.
http://thatroundhouse/

Cob can be make of many natural ingredients like clay, straw, sawdust, soil, horse hair, sand, and water. These ingredients are mixed together by hand, or foot, or machine and the resulting mix is used as a mortar to embed the log ends. The center cavity is then filled and you basically have a traditional cordwood wall without the Portland cement.

Cob is not a good insulator, but the insulation cavity of a normal cordwood wall gives the builder the option of using basically free materials from which to produce a mortar.

6.9 This is a cobwood outhouse made with log ends and cob in the forests of New Jersey by Marcus Grossman. It has a stone foundation and a living roof. Cob has a big upside and should be considered when contemplating cordwood. The best sources of information are from traditional cobbers like Ianto Evans and cobworks.com and greenbuilding.com with Clarke Snell.

Insulation Choices

The traditional insulation for use in the center cavity with cordwood construction is sawdust mixed with lime. This works well and gives an R-value of about 1.50 to 2.00 per inch, depending on your source of information. Over the years people have used: styrofoam beads, vermiculite, fiberglass, cellulose and of course the trusty sawdust/lime.

Some new options have developed:

1. **Open cell foam** (Icynene_{tm})

This has mainly been used on double wall cordwood. The outer wall of cordwood goes up first, sometimes a 'grabber lath' is placed to hold the sprayed on foam and then a second row of cordwood log ends is erected on the inside. Alan Stankevitz used this on his double wall home, as did Bruce and Nancy Kilgore. Cliff Shockey and Clint Cannon have used fiberglass batts between their double walls.

2. **Closed cell foam**

This type of foam hardens in 90 seconds and forms a vapor barrier when dried. It was first used by Sandy Clidaras of Quebec (see article on "Log Preparation, Foam Insulation, Single wall & Double wall" in the next section of this book). With his instruction and consultation, it was used on the White Earth Home in Naytahwaush, Minnesota. This type of DIY insulation comes in two twenty pound cylinders. The contents of the two cylinders are mixed through a clear plastic line with a nozzle and are injected into the wall cavity. See Addendum 1 at the back of this book on *White Earth Reservation Home* to see the process in detail.

3. **Hemp hurds**

Hemp hurds are the waste products from the industrial hemp plant. They are usually used as animal bedding in Canada where it is legal to grow industrial hemp. We used a practice batch of industrial hemp herds mixed with hydrated lime in the insulation cavity at the Cordwood Entrance Kiosk at the University of Manitoba during the Cordwood Conference in 2011. They worked very well and compressed effectively. We also used the hemp in the mortar mix with good results. The only complaint was that the hemp hurd fibers are quite long (compared to sawdust) and they can show prominently in the mortar when tuck pointing.

Practice Buildings

I have become an advocate of building a small cordwood structure BEFORE starting a house. This is the place to experiment with mortaring, tuck

pointing, mortar mixes, types of wood, sawdust, stones, special effects, etc. before trying them on your house. A little later I will discuss a

pressure treated cordwood building that can be built as small (or large) as necessary to practice the technique.

(Above)Two wonderful learning projects: A dog or cat house on the left or a small shed on the right. Both were built by Tom Huber, cordwood builder "par excellence" (T. Huber)

6.10 Some friends of ours (Dan & Kristen) hosted a workshop after the Cordwood Conference 2005. Their desire was to build a storage/maple syrup shed. With their two little helpers and loads of friendly labor they got their wish.

6.11 A practice wall made of a framework of 2" x 8"s and 8" cordwood log ends. The shelf is a 16" long slab laid up like regular cordwood. This is an excellent way to practice mixing, mortaring, tuck pointing and finishing under a top plate.

Formulas for Estimating Amounts of Materials

The following formulas are courtesy of the University of Manitoba's Engineering Department. These formulas are to help you in determining how much <u>mortar, cement, sand and hydrated lime you'll need</u>:

MORTAR: When the mix is 6 parts sand, 2 parts Portland cement and 1 part hydrated lime:

Sand: no. sq. ft. x .18 = cubic ft. of sand

Portland cement: no. sq. ft. x .063 = bags of cement

Lime: no. sq. ft. x .029 = bags of lime

MORTAR: When the mix is 5 parts sand and 2 parts masonry cement:

Sand: no. sq. ft. x .18 = cubic ft. of sand

Masonry cement: no. sq. ft. x .1= bags of cement

Use a cement mixer, wheel barrow and mortar hoe, or mortar box. Each has their special pros and cons but, on those group work days, a motorized mixer will make the walls rise much faster and save your body for mortaring and tuck pointing.

Mortar Cracking

Some cordwood masons have reported having their mortar develop hairline cracks as the walls "set up" and "dry out." There are many possible reasons for this problem.

Remember, the KEY concept in masonry, is to SLOW the SET of the MORTAR. <u>According to the masonry experts, mortar takes approximately two weeks to fully cure, so according to their advice, it is important to cover the walls for a minimum of 7 days</u>.

To do this:

- Use a correct ratio of wet/soaked sawdust in the mortar mix.
- "Mud up" your walls out of the drying rays of the sun (put up a temporary tarp if the sun is shining on your work area.)
- Don't use too many rough-cut, squared timbers in your walls (the rough cut fibers soak up moisture from the mortar very quickly).
- Don't tuck point more than twice (it weakens the mortar).
- Cover the walls with tarps, plastic, blankets, etc. when finished for the day and leave the tarps on for at least 7 days.

Chapter 7 How to Build a Cordwood Wall
Laying Up a Wall (3 sand, 2+ soaked sawdust, 1 Portland, 1 Lime)

7.1 Keep your mortar beads at 3" to 4" depending on the wall thickness. If you are using a 16" log end: a 4" mortar bead + 8" insulated cavity + 4" bead of mortar works very well.

It is important to keep the beads even and uniform to insure a good thermal resistance without an energy "nose bleed." After you have set your mortar beads, insulate the cavity.

7.2 After your first two mortar beads are down, place your first row of log ends on the mortar. Wiggle them gently to "seat" them in the mortar. Use a random pattern in your wall, do not put all log ends of the same size.

7.3 Then comes another layer of mortar. This is where it is so critical to keep the mortar beads even. You will need to pay careful attention to maintaining a continuously even mortar bead so that the R-value remains constant. Don't let mortar fall into the cavity.

tamp the sawdust

7.4 Next add some more insulation and pack it down. Some folks use a stick, others their fingers. However you do it, get it close to level with the mortar beads and then add more log ends.
(R. Flatau)

7.5 Continue in the proper order: Mortar, Insulation, Log Ends.

Use the acronym MILE to remember the correct order: Mortar, Insulation, Log Ends.

7.6 Then it is time to tuck point the mortar. Push the mortar back ½ inch and smooth around it with a spoon, bent butter knife, or masonry tool.

knife

What makes cordwood different from brick and block masonry is the random patterning of the log ends. It is of the utmost importance to use logs of all different shapes and sizes in the walls. This not only strengthens the mortar joints, but it also makes for an attractive looking wall. If a special pattern is desired with log ends or bottle ends, it can be planned ahead of time, laid out on the floor and then placed in the wall as it rises. See the section in the Cordwood Cabin addendum of this book for pictures of the Big Dipper wall at the Cordwood Education Center.

Keeping the wall level and plumb is not only an aesthetic preference it is a structural imperative as well.   A plumb bob, a mason's line, a four foot mason's level, or a swinging 1" x 4" plumb bob (from the top plate) can help keep your wall straight. Step back and check every few rows to see that you are maintaining a straight wall and a random pattern. Sometimes the log ends may vary as much as an inch in length (if you haven't done due diligence when bucking them up) and so it becomes essential to keep either the interior of the exterior wall plumb. Most cordwood builders settle on keeping the interior walls straight and level..

A random pattern starts with the first row.

Plumb bob

When mortaring a wall, there are a few key points to keep in mind:

1. Always build horizontally-one row at a time. If you build up one corner too high the whole wall may slip (mortar slump).
2. Logs should not touch. Keep at least 1" space between logs. Tuck point around each log; do not let the mortar slump in the center and touch—result: energy nosebleed.

keyway

Keying the Mortar

7.9 Cordwood builders are now advocating using a "keyway" or a vertical piece of 1" x 1" secured to each side of the post. The keyway idea came from cordwood buildings in earthquake prone regions. The keyway has been found to reduce air infiltration. It is important that the mortar bead 'grab' the keyway.

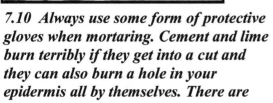

7.10 Always use some form of protective gloves when mortaring. Cement and lime burn terribly if they get into a cut and they can also burn a hole in your epidermis all by themselves. There are many types of masonry gloves on the market. Choose ones that work for you. Rubbing Petroleum Jelly on your hands before the gloves gives extra protection against mortar burns.

Cold Weather Mortaring

Many have asked the question: "Can I mortar when it is going to freeze at night?" The answer is NO. If the water in the mortar mix freezes the mortar will not properly set and it will crumble.

According to the masonry experts mortar takes at least 14 days to cure. So it will be important to watch the weather and either "hurry up and finish," postpone the mortaring, or provide heat and cover for the mortar. Using blankets, tarps and plastic will help for a few days, especially if the daytime temperatures will rise above freezing.

LPM (Lime Putty Mortar) takes a full month to set up and cure, so plan the mortaring portion of your project well if using this slow curing mortar.

The current literature advises against adding any "retarder" or additive to the mortar to make it slow down its set or to keep it from freezing. The best natural additive to do this is the soaked sawdust. Cordwood builders I have spoken with have been dissatisfied with the mortar additives and retarders they have tried. If you plan on using anything other than what is advised, please build a test wall to before you try it on your home.

Note: Ross Martinek, a Licensed Professional Geologist wrote a 13 page article for the *Cordwood Conference Papers 2005*, entitled "Moving Mud." In it he defines all the various details a builder should know about mortar. He explains additives, retarders, cold weather mortaring and the aggregates involved in mortar and cement. It is a worthwhile "read" and one that will give a cordwood mason a better understanding of the masonry medium.

7.10a Summer, our cordwood workshop supervisor/greeter, sits in repose after a very successful cordwood workshop in New London, Minnesota. The beautiful, random pattern cordwood walls are the result of good listeners and avid workers. (R. Flatau)

Random Pattern

7.11 A beautiful random pattern wall by Jim Piontkowski.

Keep a random pattern in your wall, don't put in all the same shape and size logs. A random pattern wall just looks so "darn good."

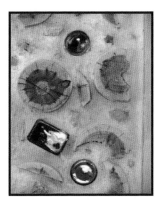

7.12 Random pattern with bottle ends.

Tuck Pointing (more pointers)

As the wall rises and you go up three logs, go back down to the bottom and smooth the mortar around each log. This doesn't take as long as it sounds, and it helps to not only make the wall look nicer but actually strengthens the mortar joint. If you are going to leave the logs exposed, it is worth your while to "point" the logs. Using a butter knife or spoon will help with the process, but your gloved fingers will work just as well. You may choose to recess the mortar to let the logs "stand proud". I've used each method in different rooms of my home and both have a pleasing effect, although the recessed TUCK POINTED logs make a more dramatic visual display.

7.13 Using the "karate chop" part of your hand to tuck point (this way there are no finger prints in the mortar.)

Each log should be tuck pointed so the mortar is recessed 1/2" - 1". When you are finished for the day (or night) it is important to slow down the set of the mortar so it will not crack or shrink. Covering the finished section with blankets,

87

tarps, or plastic is the best way to slow down the set. Hosing down the wall, the way you would a slab is not advised because the lime and Portland cement will leach out and stain the log ends. When you return the next day and need to work on a half-finished wall, wet down the last course of mortar and log ends from the previous days work. This will help the new mortar adhere better and won't wick moisture away from the new batch. This is where keeping your mortar mix ratios accurate is important. I have seen too many cordwood walls where it was clearly evident where one day's work stopped (dark mortar) and the next started (different shade of mortar.

7.14 Tuck pointing with a butter knife with a curved (bent) blade, or a spoon gives a smoother surface to the mortar.

Once all your walls are up and you're ready to move in—DON'T—not at least until you've wired brushed the wall to remove all the excess mortar.

A shop-vac and a dust mask are essential tools for this project. It is much easier to brush and vacuum the walls before the tile, carpet and furniture is in place. Plan on having to go back in a year or so to caulk and chink any gaps or checks that have opened. This is to be expected and not a cause for alarm. "Primary Checks" in the logs are best stuffed

with white fiberglass insulation (some folks use brown paper bags or oakum). Use a butter knife to force the insulation deep in the cavity. Go outside and do the same thing, because a primary check runs all the way through. This is a natural part of maintenance of a cordwood home.

7.15 Leaving your work at "days end." This is called "setting the teeth."
Note how the mortar is set at the same level as the log ends.
Do not set a mortar bead <u>above</u> the top of the log ends. (R. Flatau)

Coming back to work on a **"set teeth wall"** is lovingly called, "**filling the teeth.**" Wet the mortar and log ends in preparation for the fresh mortar bead. Then start with the **M.I.L.E.** chant (**mortar, insulation, log end**).

Cold Mortar Joints 'Filling the Teeth' Getting ready for the next days work.

7.18 Here a brush has been dipped in a pail of water and the mortar beads and the exposed log ends that will receive a new mortar bead, are brushed with water. This helps the new mortar from being "sucked dry" by the curing mortar. (Flatau)

Note the bottle ends set into the wall. They have been held together with duct tape. The clear glass goes **outside** and colored glass goes on the **inside.** This will give the best light for your labor.

7.16 On the left: An example of setting a bottle end in the wall. This set of two bottles in a 12" wall has an aluminum plate wrapped around it and secured with duct tape. This will help sunlight to travel to the inside and light up the colored bottle end.

7.17 On the right: 16" bottle end making using various methods: duct tape, aluminum tape, and "handi coils." Note: the neck sticks through the clear bottle. (R. Flatau)

Cleaning the mortar after mortaring

It is important to clean up the excess mortar that gets left on the log ends, the posts, the floor and seemingly everywhere. The mortar can be easily cleaned while it has not fully dried, but if you don't have the opportunity to do that, you can wire brush it later.

7.19 Cleaning up the mortar that inevitably gets on the log ends, posts and beams. A wire brush works very well as does a wire wheel on a drill. Make sure to wear eye protection and a dust mask while doing this, since mortar dust will be flying everywhere.. (R. Flatau)

My wife came up with a great idea for cleaning the inside log end faces.   In certain situations, the interior log end faces are cleaned up with a chop saw just before mortaring. These faces often are smooth and clean.   Becky used Murphy's Oil Soap to wipe them off after they had been cleaned with a wire brush. These were Tamarack logs which have a two-tone coloring. The Murphy's oil soap made the colors stand out.   Do not use this method if the log faces are rough cut with a chain saw.

Step Back from the Wall

Step away from your project every so often and make sure you are:

- Maintaining constant mortar joints
- Building with a random pattern
- Keeping the wall level and plumb
- Putting in bottle ends or shelves or special effects where you want them
- Checking both sides of the wall, not just the one you are working on presently
- Using the pattern: Mortar, Insulation, Log End (in that order) MILE
- Cleaning your tools at the end of the day
- Tarping your walls to prevent rapid drying of the mortar
- Don't finish the day with mortar on top of the log ends

Electrical

The electrical wiring needs to be run before the mortar is put in place, so it is advisable to have a wiring plan drawn. There are many different ways to tackle the wiring plan. **Above all, "keep to the letter of the law" with electrical codes. Don't skimp or shortcut on wiring.** It is such an important part of your home and it requires care to install wiring **safely**. Here are a few things that cordwood owner/builders have used:

- Conduit allows you to run the metal or plastic conduit first and then "fish" your wires through later.
- Or put the conduit in and run the wires at the same time. Wires can be replaced at any time in the future.
- UF 12-2 underground wire. In my post and beam home all the wiring in the exterior walls runs in the middle of the posts (between the mortar beads) and is held on with wire staples.
- Metal cable wire is also an easy way to wire a house safely.
- All your receptacles, junction boxes, and light outlets will need to be put in placed before you mortar. So whatever your code calls for, get it set up and installed before "slinging mud."

7.20 Note the conduit is run to the top of the ceiling, where it is then joined with other wires. In this instance there is an outside receptacle and an inside one. Note that the boxes have been foamed to reduce air infiltration. (R. Flatau)

7.21 Electrical with 14-2 (yellow) wire-stapled to the inside of a double-posted framework. Also note the keyways running vertically up each post. The mortar will be "grabbed" by the keyways.

Windows & window boxes

Each window in a cordwood building must have a "window box." The window box will be built out of dimensional lumber, the width of the cordwood wall (for example: a 16" cordwood wall you will need two 2" x 8" boxes). The window box will then be braced to keep it square. The window slides into this window box and is fastened.

NOTE: Make a "dry run" by putting the actual window into the window box BEFORE you secure it to the frame or float it in the cordwood wall. That way you will have no surprises/tight fits when it comes time to set your windows in the fastened window boxes.

There are basically 3 ways to place a window box and hence a window in a cordwood wall.

7.22 (Above) If you are choosing stackwall or round (without posts) you need to float your window in the mortar matrix as your wall reaches window height. If your window is large and heavy or will span a large section of wall, you need to put a wooden timber (called a lintel) both under and in some cases of extreme weight, over the window.

7.23 This window box (right) is made of two 2" x 8"s. It is screwed to the top plate and braced diagonally. Note If you are using posts and beams or timber framing, the second method and the third are basically the same. In the one scenario the window box is attached to the posts. The posts have been accurately placed to receive the window box. The window box may also be nailed or screwed to a beam running in between the posts. Oftentimes for a large window there is a beam above and below.

7.24 The third way is to attach the braced window box to the top plate or to side post. The wood screws are then secured into the top plate/posts with a drill.

Here is a window box with an interior template (diagonal) for accuracy in measurement..

Maintenance on a cordwood home

There are a few maintenance tasks that a cordwood home owner must undertake. Like any home, the owner must do an annual visual inspection. This involves a few things:

- Walk around the exterior of the home looking at the cordwood from top to bottom.
- Look for log shrinkage, mortar shrinkage or large checks that have developed.
- Look for mortar cracks.
- Look for any discoloration of the log ends.
- Check for insect presence or damage
- . Do the same on the interior walls.

If you live in a cold climate, it is helpful to walk around the interior on a cold winter's day and put your hand against the log ends to see if there is any air infiltration. After one year heating there may be some log ends that have checked or dried and left small gaps. These gaps can be easily filled. We have used:

- White fiberglass for the checks that develop in the round log ends (stuff the checks with white fiberglass using a butter knife or screwdriver—do this on the interior & exterior). White fiberglass matches the color of the mortar and is formaldehyde free.

  For log shrinkage, mortar shrinkage, and cracking:
- Log shrinkage can be handled with Permachink, Log Jam, or clear silicone caulk. .These more expensive caulks last for many years.
- Permachink and Log Jam come in mortar colors. Both products are water soluble and clean up well (IF you clean them up right away) otherwise the caulk sticks like glue the next day.

After a number of years and depending on how much sun, rain or snow hit your log ends; there may be discoloration or darkening of the log ends. This can be handled in a number of ways:

- Do nothing. Some people like the natural aging of a log end and gray or dark coloration are simply manifestations of aging wood.
- Treat the exterior log end face with a UV blocker. The UV blocker must also be breathable, so that the log end can transpire moisture.
- Permachink makes a breathable log stain called Lifeline Exterior (breathable, transparent, mildew resistant, water repellant, UV protection, soap/water clean-up, environmentally friendly and, alas, expensive). We used the Light stain #120 on posts, beams, window boxes and log ends on the exterior of the Cordwood Education Center
- If you have not stained your log ends, you can take a belt sander, an angle grinder or a drill with a sanding pad and simply sand off the gray/dark discoloration.

Chapter 8   Bottle Ends & Special Effects

8.1 (Right)) Mike and Honey Amman have done some amazing things with recycled bottles.

With bottle ends or stones you will need to clean them at the end of the mortaring day or they will be stained.

8.2 (Left) Tom and Marcy Melvig have added a chakra bottle end wall to their lovely home in Hancock, Michigan. (R. Flatau)

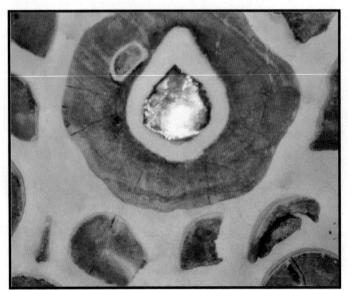

8.3 John Meilahn has done all kinds of wonderful things in his cordwood home in Michigan. Here is a polished copper agate mortared into a hollowed cedar log end. (R. Flatau)

(See the article on making bottle ends in Addendum 2 *Cordwood Cabin*)

Special Effects

8.4 Mermaid Cottage in Del Norte, Colorado. The bottle end motifs within a post & beam framework are especially attractive.

8.5 The tree at the left is mortared into the wall. The mortar and bottle ends are infilled around it. The mortar is cleaned and the tree is sealed with a breathable, clear stain. (K. Cellura-Shields)

8.6 A timber framed entrance. The stained glass on the right of the door is simply framed with dimensional lumber. The stained glass was placed in the frame after the walls were erected.(Flatau)

Chapter 9   Other Considerations & Ideas

Log Preparation, Foam Insulation, Single wall & Double wall

Sandy & Angelika Clidaras

*Author's note: Cordwood is a building technique that is ever evolving and improving. Even though the technique is fairly simple there are a myriad of different ideas about how to accomplish the task of building a log-end wall. Sandy has graciously given a straight forward, honest presentation which summarizes his **log prep, foam insulation** and his considerations on **single and double wall options**. I would advise anyone interested in Sandy's technique to visit his website (listed below).*

- **Log Preparation**
  The "prevention approach" to log shrinkage
- **Single Log Wall Foam Insulation**
  Advantages
- **Single or Double Log Cordwood Wall?**

My name is **Sandy Clidaras. Angelica** (my wife) and I built our cordwood home in Quebec, Canada. We began researching cordwood in 1995 & have been in our Cordwood home since Nov 2004. On our web site, **"The Cordstead"**, we have available our **Cordstead Memoirs & Research Corner,** where there are full reports on these subjects.

9.1 The new garage at the Clidaras Cordstead. (Sandy Clidaras)
http://thecordstead.blogspot.com/

Log Preparation – The prevention approach to log shrinkage.

How does that old saying go? "An ounce of prevention is worth a pound of cure."

Cordwood has been plagued with logs shrinking in the mortar wall making for drafty air leaks and heat loss. The type of wood, drying time, rot resistance, log size (diameter), & log treatment, all play a big roll in controlling shrinkage.

Type of wood – I recommend using stable soft woods with the highest rot resistance available to you. They are more forgiving with mortar joints, unlike some hardwoods.

Drying time –It takes at least 2 years air-drying to reach Equilibrium Moisture Content. You can't over dry them. I recommend getting your logs prepped & drying as soon as possible.

Log Size – Keep diameters to 8" or less to help speed up drying time and minimize shrinkage. Smaller diameters are usually lighter to work with, cheaper to buy, and easier to find.

Log treatment – Wood is like a sponge. Mortar needs to stay wet to cure properly & not crack. When you place a dry log in a wet mortar mix, two things happen. The wood takes on water and starts to swell in the wet mortar, pushing back the still soft mortar. Once the log dries, it shrinks back down & may loosen in the mortar. Another detrimental thing is that if the mortar dries too fast, it can possibly loose strength and crack.

We applied a water repellant type of product (like Thompson's water seal) to treat the logs **only on the two 4 ½" ends where the logs contact the mortar and NOT THE ENTIRE LOG.** The idea is to prevent the water transfer between the log and the mortar.

9.2 Sandy Clidaras's log preparation.

I also used a log prep that involved mixing borax and propylene glycol to preserve and help it penetrate into the logs. Dunking them in a tank was a long term solution and allowed the borax to penetrate into the wood. Four cups borax, one gallon of warm water and one gallon of glycol were heated & mixed in a large pot. Then the logs were dunked for a minute. Next the log ends were sealed with a moisture permeable latex-based stain, which allows the logs to breathe. The entire method is described in detail in my article in the ***Cordwood Conference Papers 2005, "Log-end Treatment and Insulation Techniques."***

Having lived in our cordwood home since 2004, we have no loose logs. However there are many fine crack lines in the mortar (nothing serious) in several wall areas. Most were noted on the south side and I believe they were caused from the weather at the time of building (sun, heat and wind exposure).

Mortar Mix—load bearing walls

The main house has some fine line mortar cracks, mostly on the (lakeside) windy, south, sunny side. This main house was "brush finished."

3 – Masons sand
1 - Soaked sawdust
1 – 1 mortar cement
1 – Masons lime

After the Cordwood Conference 2005 and having spoken with both Jack Henstridge and Ross Martinek we decided to try another mix. For the garage we tried this mix, (a somewhat coarser look). This was also **"brush finished."**

---

2 - Masons sand
1 – ¼" Crushed clean gravel (not the smooth pea gravel)
1 - Soaked sawdust
1 – Portland Cement
1 – Masons Lime

We found that this mix was less likely to slump so we didn't have to go back as often to re-point and, so far, has fewer fine line cracks. It is a little darker in color, coarser looking and was also a little easier to mix as the gravel helped keep things stirred up in the mixer.

Single Log Wall Foam Insulation – advantages.

After considering options, we chose to inject closed cell foam in our wall cavity. It is costly, safe, easy to install, and available in do-it-your self kits.

Advantages are that the foam expands in irregular shaped cavities filling in all cracks and making an airtight seal. It has a high R-value (R-7) per inch making for a well insulated wall. This allows the use of shorter logs & narrower footings & stem walls, cutting costs and materials. 5"to 7" of foam can yield an insulation value of R-35 to R-49.

The foam bonds well to wood and mortar, and has a light elasticity. It also acts as a vapor barrier and will not absorb moisture, rot, mold or mildew. It will not settle or leak out of the cavity. The insulating values are not lost if it gets wet and it is not food for insects or rodents.

9.3 The foam insulation being installed. (S. Clidaras)

Foam is available in large do-it-yourself kits not requiring any heavy equipment or special tooling, allowing you to control and oversee the installation to insure a complete coverage in the installation process.

This foam is expensive, but is getting more popular and the pricing is becoming more competitive. The wall in our single-story 40-foot round house cost almost $4,000 Canadian, including 15% tax. Costs will vary by location.

In my opinion, super insulating with foam creating an air tight sealed wall is a one-time fixed financial investment. The insulation requires no maintenance (no loose or moving pieces), and will last the lifetime of the building, saving you energy costs, and making for a more comfortable & enjoyable home environment.

When you consider the tremendous energy cost saving over the life of your home, closed cell foam can be well worth the investment.

Single or Double Log Cordwood Wall? – Comparison

Wall configurations – I used these examples for comparison.

Single Log Wall – 1 log 18", set 1½" proud of the mortar. 2 rows of 4½" of mortar creating a 6" cavity in the center spanned by logs tying the mortar rows together. 6" cavity is injected with closed cell foam insulation. By surface area, the logs make up 60% & mortar 40%.

Double Log Wall - 2 of 8" logs (16"), 2 walls (one inner & one outer . Outer wall is built, then the entire wall is sprayed with 5 ½" open cell foam insulation, and then the inner wall is built. Total wall thickness is approximately 22". At least 2 rows of 3" mortar **per wall**, if not (PEM or mortar) the entire 8" length through. Total 12" of mortar or 14" PEM (Logs 1" proud). Logs are 70% of wall area & mortar 30%.

It really boils down to how you personally feel about it and how much time, labor, material, & money you are willing to invest.

I have not built a double log cordwood wall but have tried to make an honest comparison without favoring any one building system.

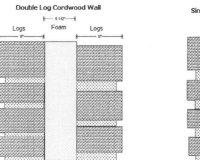
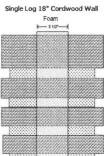

Let's look at the differences.

Logs
Labor – Double log wall - twice the cutting, & setting in wall(s). Shorter logs can be difficult to keep plumb & also (depending on local code requirements), Post & beam, & or bracing, strapping, or backing (plywood/ particle board) may be needed = Extra time & expense. wear & tear on equipment, fuel/energy, blades/chains for saw(s).

Material – Single log wall - 2.5% more logs, adjusting 2" length & 10% for wall area.

Mortar
Material – Double log wall – 43.75% - 64.7% more mortar or PEM.

Labor – Double log wall - 43.75% – 64.75% more mortar mixing. Double laying up of mortar (2 Walls). 1 ½ times the pointing, as you still have to point the inside once, to level the log & make a tight seal.

Consider the extra wear & tear on equipment, Cement/ Mortar mixers, tools, etc., extra energy/fuel to operate this equipment, extra time required, Extra weight of the wall (load on footing).

Insulation
Single Log Wall – 40% of wall area is mortar.
Double Log Wall – Entire wall surface area 100%.
Material – Double log wall –Insulated by area **(60%)** more foam required. Open Cell foam difference by volume in order to obtain an equal R-factor is 46 %.
These percentages do not reflect on cost differences.
Single Log Wall - Costs per board foot for DIY (Do it yourself) Closed Cell Foam installation kits are higher than hiring an insulation contractor for a one-time installation visit installation.

R-Values
Single Log Wall– average R-factor = **R 33.62**
Double Log Wall – Average R-Value **R-37.8**, using PEM a little higher **R-40**.
R-Factors -Single Log Wall has R 4.48 - R 6.38 **less than the Double Log Wall**

Other Considerations
Double Log Wall – Cost for deeper window & doorframes –(thicker walls). Building up off of the ground requires a wider knee wall.
Single Log Wall - insulation cavity can be easily enlarged to increase the insulation value by leaving the logs less proud, moving the mortar rows, adding 1" more foam, & still use an 18"log.
   Depending on codes, in some areas, you **do not** have to build with a Post & Beam frame, so you can build a load bearing cordwood wall, simplifying the plans & eliminating substantial material costs & labor.

My Conclusion

Building codes here (Montreal, Canada) require a minimum R-20 wall & this single log wall at R 33.62 is **168%** of that requirement.
When do you have enough? Is there is a point, in insulating a wall, where the return on investment is practically nil?
   A Double Wall log end home will have more mass, weight, insulation R- factor, use more material, need more labor, cost more & requires a lot more time to build.
   Either of these 2 methods will produce a well insulated, air tight cordwood wall with superior insulation values, compared to most generic stick frame built homes, if built correctly.
   There are many wall configurations possible in both single & double log cordwood walls. That makes this look at the 2 methods limited to these design specs, and this comparison for use as a general over view.

Thank you Sandy for the concise summary of your exceptional methods; I would encourage everyone who is investigating cordwood to research Sandy's techniques.
http://thecordstead.blogspot.com/

Top Plate

The top plate is already in place on the post and beam framework home. It is important to **double** the top plate for added strength and roof support on a post and beam home. Put some caulk or a gasket between the two plates to reduce air infiltration. Another top plate option is to use native sawn lumber or an LVL (laminated veneer lumber).

For those who build round or stackwall, the top plates are tied in as the final course rises. Mortar must be leveled and the top plate put in place. The top plate can be dimensional lumber equaling the width of your wall (two 2"x 8's for a 16" wall.) It is helpful to bend 5" spikes every 8 to 12 inches. This will help the mortar grab and set the plate in place. Some builders have reported having difficulty with leveling the top plate with just bent spikes. One such builder, Brian McGrath of Brownfield, Maine, suggests using a threaded rod or rebar, which goes down several courses into the cordwood wall (this would have to be put into place when you are four or five courses from the top). The top plate would then be placed on top of the rods, pounded with a hammer to make the appropriate indentations for drilling (similar to how anchor bolts are used on a foundation).

5.5 Top Plates - *Wind and Anchorage*

Top plates are installed at both the exterior and interior of the wall and serve to tie in the roof. The top plates can be made from 2x4s laid in a bed of mortar, held in place with anchor bolts. If additional strength is desired, use 2x6s held in place with anchor bolts.

Set the top plates into 1 to 2 inches of mortar and tap level. Figure 5.23 illustrates a typical system of top plates.

In addition to snow loads on roof structures that create forces that push down on the wall, there are wind forces that may act in an opposite manner. These forces can cause uplift on the roof system, which in turn pull up on the wall. To resist the uplift it is important the top plates are anchored well within the wall. Figure 5.23 details the top-plate anchorage system that we recommend. The anchor bolts are fabricated from 3/8 - inch diameter rod with 6 inches of thread at the end that goes through the plate. Once you are about 2-1/2 feet from the top of the wall lay in log ends that have been prepared as shown in Figure 5.22.

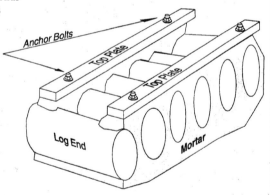

Fig. 5.22: **Installation of Top Plates**

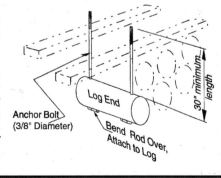

Holes would be drilled to allow the top plate to make contact with the mortar and the top plate would then be screwed into place. The threaded rod should make it easier to level the top plate for your roof.

9.4 The drawing to the left is how the University of Manitoba ties the top plate into the rest of the cordwood wall, when building using the stackwall method. This drawing and explanation are courtesy of Dr. Kris Dick, PEng. From his book Stackwall: How to Build It.

101

9.5 Some have built a scale model to show door, window, roof placement and visual appearance. (J. Henstridge)

The Roof

Once again personal tastes, preferences and financial assets come into play when deciding on how to "top" your home. A cordwood structure can be roofed in a variety of conventional or unconventional ways. Trusses, common gable, hip, shed, gambrel, geodesic dome, living roof, metal, room in the attic truss, and so forth, may all be successfully employed.

My truss, room-in-the-attic roof provided an additional 560 sq. ft. (2 bedrooms, half bath, and a playroom) at an added cost of $1200 over a common truss roof. A truss-built-roof is often times not only the most inexpensive (much less carpentry time), but also the strongest way to go. Trusses are engineered to take the considerable roof weight away from pushing outward on the walls and redirect it upward to the truss. This is usually performed with a series of strategically located triangles that are gusseted or gang-nailed to produce a significantly stronger roof. Also, because of their inherently stronger structure, it is often possible to use less of them by having them spaced 24" on center, rather than 16", with no loss of stability. I also used conventional CDX plywood: 1/2" 4 ply, roofing paper and 240 pound shingles.

Jack Henstridge and Rob Roy have both used living roofs on their homes and write glowingly of watching the grass grow. Installing a living roof requires careful, waterproofing preparation. The current literature on green roofs and waterproofing offers many different methods. I would advise that you read the current literature available on living roofs. In addition to a living roof, Jack Henstridge also built a geodesic dome and a gambrel style roof on his beautiful "ship with wings home" near Oromocto, New Brunswick,

One of the most effective techniques in determining which roof to build is to make a detailed drawing of your home using a protractor, T-square and graph paper, to give a visual approximation. (This is extremely useful in plotting room, door and window placement.) It is ever so much simpler to move an object on paper, than after it has been nailed, cemented and screwed

Some thoughtful souls even build a cardboard mock-up of the abode to give a three dimensional perspective. Use a magic marker to show windows and doors and color or paint it to approximate the finished product. If you plan to use a passive, active or direct gain solar heating system, you will want to make sure of your site location to achieve maximum solar exposure. See *The Solar House* by Dan Chiras for an excellent discussion of using solar to enhance your home.

Energy Heel Truss (High Heel Truss)

To get the maximum r-value out of your roof insulation, consider using an Energy Heel Truss (also known as a High Heel Truss). The "heel" or edge of the truss (where it makes contact with the top/bearing plate), is where most of the heat escapes from the home (the other culprits are windows, doors and plumbing ingress). If you are able to install 14" of insulation (R-51) all the way to the edge of the wall, you ensure the integrity of your roofs r-value.

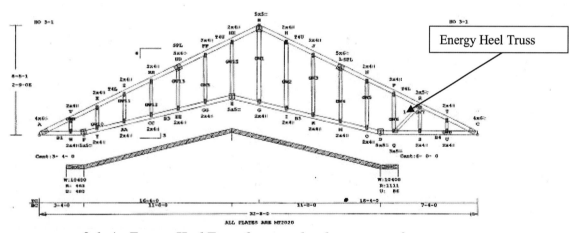

9.6 An Energy Heel Truss from our local truss manufacturer.

Room in the Attic Trusses

When we were building our home, we were fortunate to have a neighbor who managed a truss factory. When I was going to put a 4/12 pitch truss roof on my cordwood home, he suggested I look into Room-in-the-Attic trusses, which effectively gives you half of the living space of your first floor. We went from 1200 sq. ft. to 1800 sq. ft. with an application that cost nearly the same as a regular truss. It usually costs less to build on top of a building, so for cash strapped folks (like us) this was an excellent way to have more space for our growing family. The one caveat with this configuration is that the "run" from the knee walls to the upper attic space has room for only 6" of fiberglass. The newer trusses on the market offer a double wall truss that gives up to R-40 in that same space.

Here is a diagram of our room in the attic truss. Use it as an example only and see what your local building supply store has to offer.

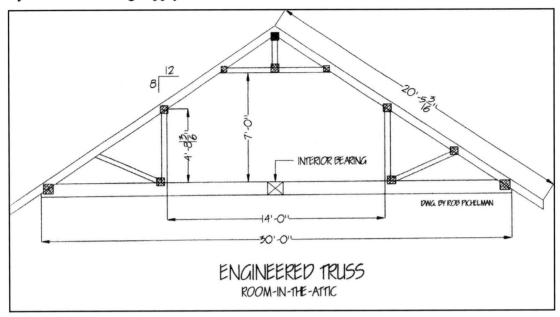

ENGINEERED TRUSS
ROOM-IN-THE-ATTIC

9.7   Room in the attic trusses gave an extra 560 sq. ft. of living space and allowed for two bedrooms, a half bath and a den.

Plumbing

Since these choices vary so distinctly with each climate and setting, one should read everything available on heating, plumbing, wiring, basic framing, layout, earth sheltering, solar, photovoltaics, masonry, carpentry (rough and finish), site selection and layout, etc. to satisfy your personal taste. Every home becomes a very special extension of one's lifestyle, personality and philosophy, it is important to understand all the available options. The public library or the internet are fine places to begin.

As to what we did:

- We used copper for our hot and cold water and ran all the plumbing (except for the waste and venting) along the ceiling joists. The pipes were all covered with insulation and wrapped so they would not sweat and leak.
- We also "backed" our bath and kitchen plumbing against each other, to save money on long plumbing runs.
- The 1st floor bathroom plumbing is further utilized to reach the upstairs bathroom directly above the downstairs one. Plan your home wisely.
- We put in a domestic solar hot water system using Wisconsin's Focus on Energy Rebates. Ours has two 4' x 8' Heliodyne thermal hot water panels, complete with pumps and 80 gallon pre-heat tank. We love our system and are saving dollars every time the sun shines.

Finishing

The cordwood can be left as is, inside and out, and as this book's pictures illustrate, the visual effect is distinctive, impressive and unique. Some of the older cordwood homes have been covered. The Northern Housing Committee of the University of Manitoba advocates keeping one wall (either exterior or interior) as straight and level as possible for eventual finishing. I feel that, having lived in a cordwood home for 30+ years, covering up a wall would ruin the intriguing pattern of cedar and close off the fresh aromatic scent that still pervades our abode. But, dear reader, the final decision rests with you.

HVAC

The current literature on cordwood often includes mention of the use of radiant-in-floor heating. This is an excellent source of "heat at your feet." Pex tubing has become more reasonably priced and there are many contractors who will let you help or, if you are so inclined, do it yourself. I had a "Rule of Three" when building, that is, I would talk to three contractors before I made a decision. Often I would ask the contractor if he/she would let me work with his/her crew as a helper or a "gopher." Many said "no," some said "yes," I went with those who let me help. Be upfront, I told them I was poor and was looking to save a buck, but wanted to do things properly.

We have a large Hearthstone wood stove in the center of the house. We love it and it provides 100% of our heat if we need it and stoke it. We also have a 75,000 BTU backup propane furnace for when we "go on vacation" in the winter or when we are too lazy to put a log on the fire. Baseboard electric provides a fail safe for winter vacations. It is never used otherwise. Finally we have a 20' wall of insulated solar room glass to capture solar heat during the cold, sunny days of winter. The floor is the heat sink and it is insulated with extruded styrofoam, with paving brick and concrete on top.

Do your homework on the heating, ventilation and air conditioning systems. Cordwood's thermal mass can certainly help decrease the amount of energy your home consumes, but you need to size your heating and cooling needs to meet current code levels. Thinking about resale is not necessarily a negative way of thinking. Plan for the worst, expect the best.

Decisions, Decisions [So many decisions to make]

When deciding to build with cordwood, a word of advice. Take your time and do your research. There are many ideas about how to build a cordwood wall, what type of wood to use, what type of mortar, foundation, wiring, roof, windows, heating system, etc. Each of these cordwood building questions requires an answer. It is better to read, talk, ponder and then decide, than to blindly follow any author or builder's ideas. Give yourself time to take a cordwood workshop, build a practice building, try out the different mortar mixes, ask questions on the Daycreek.com forum, call a cordwood builder and go visit some cordwood homes. In other words, do your research and then you can answer these questions for yourself.

Cracks, Log Loosening & Permachinktm

What happens when a log or two loosens up in your wall? No need for alarm, this is an

expected condition with cordwood. It is a cosmetic problem and sometimes a heat-loss problem (if the loosened log end lets in cold outside air). The problem is easily fixed with the use of Permachinktm or Log Jamtm. Both products are similar and work the same way. They are comprised of a co-acrylic polymer that moves with the wood and mortar. The most common application is for horizontal log cabins as chinking between the logs.

9.8 A five gallon bucket of Permachink and a "hand" water sprayer.

The first step is to determine if you have to seal just one or two logs or a whole wall section. When I was doing a wall section that had quite a few loose log ends and some large checks, I decided to apply Permachink to the entire 8' x 8' section of mortar.

Here is how I did it: First of all, it is important to cover the floor and anything else that might get "Perma-chinked." This stuff has some serious sticking power. Get a water mister and a pair of rubber gloves.

The next step is to cover some of the protruding log ends. My log ends stand proud about ¾ of an inch. Take masking tape and cover as many as you can or want to. If you don't, rest assured that some of the Permachink will "stick like glue" to the log end.

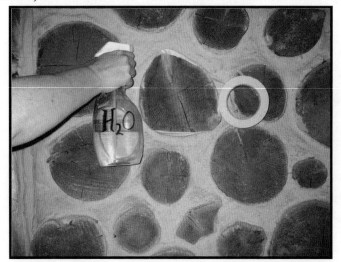

Next it is important to "mist" the wall section you are going to work on with water. No need to drown the wall or the mortar, just get it moist. A spray bottle works very well. Wash it out with soap and water first and then adjust the nozzle to light spray. There is no need to get the log ends wet. The water helps the Permachink to stick to the mortar and where the log end attaches to the mortar.

9.9 Spray around the mortar first. This helps the Permachink adhere to the mortar.

106

Then slather a handful of PermaChink/Log Jam over the mortar and pretend you are tuck

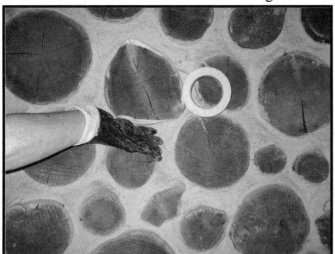

pointing. It is not necessary to put on a thick coat. Only 1/8 of an inch or so is needed. It is a messy job, but the main objective is to cover all the mortar. Permachink can be used on the inside and the outside if necessary. It also comes in caulking tubes for small jobs. The five gallon pail is quite expensive, but it covers a huge area. I mortared four 8 x 8 foot sections and still had more than 2/3's of a pail left.

9.10 The Permachink is" slathered" on, just like mortar.

Permachink has a new type of product called Chink-Paint. **Chink-Paint** is an elastomeric, textured coating for renewing or changing the color of chinking. This makes it ideal for giving a facelift to your home by brightening the appearance of the existing mortar. Chink-Paint's elasticity enables it to expand and contract with Permachink or Energy Seal without cracking or peeling. While Permachink is not breathable. Chink Paint is breathable.

Chink Paint would be applied to all the mortar before the Permachink and then the Permachink would only be applied to edge of the log ends that have developed mortar separation (i.e. log loosening). This should be a way to save money by using a less expensive product to cover the mortar. Make certain you get the same color of each product. If you don't have internet access, go to the library and they will help you use one for free.

www.permachink.com   www.sashco.com

9.11 This lovely round cordwood home has been Permachinked on every wall on the inside and out.

White fiberglass

9.12 Stuffing a gap with white fiberglass.

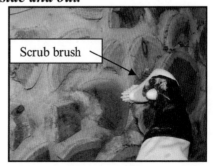

Scrub brush

9.13 Spreading with a scrub brush.

107

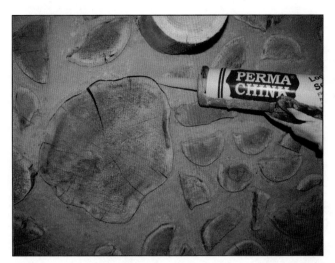

9.14 Permachink caulking, mortar colored, moves with the wood and the mortar. It is the ideal solution for log loosening or log checking.

Why don't the cordwood log ends rot?

The log ends are the key to keeping the cordwood decay-free.

- End grain acts as a "wick" to pull moisture away. The xylem and phloem act as "straws," if you will, to pull any water from the wood. It is truly amazing how quickly a wet cordwood wall dries out. This is why the log ends need to "breathe" and cannot be sealed with anything that prevents them from "breathing."
- If you do stain your log ends, make certain it is with a product that will allow moisture to transpire. If the cordwood does get wet from a driving rain or snowstorm, it will quickly dry out.

There are a few important considerations:

- Keep the log ends off the foundation with a built-up perimeter of insulated block or stone.
- Build large overhangs on your building.
- Gutter your building to prevent "splashback."
- Use only dry, barked, decay resistant softwoods.

Chapter 10

How did you become Mortgage-Free?

We used a few basic strategies to become mortgage free:

1. Get out of debt and stay out of debt. Get rid of the credit cards except for emergencies or pay off the full amount every month.
2. Establish a "Building Fund." Place part of your earnings into a fund for your project. If you happen to be looking at a distant time frame, invest it in a CD, safe Mutual Fund or Money Market Fund to accrue more interest than you would from the bank.
3. Gather equity in your current living situation. We bought a "handyman special" home and fixed it up. We made money on the sale of the house to finish our cordwood home.
4. Build "out of pocket" and don't borrow money. When we had $50 we spent $50 and not a penny more. My friends use to tease me that I would drive across the county to buy nails for a couple of pennies cheaper (they were right).
5. Stockpile materials. We had our insulation, windows, doors, wood and lime bought and safely stored, before we ever started construction at the building site.
6. Look around for bargains and discounts.
7. Recycle, refurbish and reuse. Go to local places that sell recycled items from homes. Habitat for Humanity has a great site:
   www.habitat.org/env/restores.html
   Other sites are: www.freecycle.com   www.build.recycle.net   www.satruck.com
   www.craigslist.com
8. Go to Construction sites: ask for materials that are being "tossed." Go to landfills, garage sales, "trash & treasure" days (where items are picked up for free by the city dump trucks.)
9. Don't spend more than you have.
10. If you can live on your building site in a trailer, RV, tent or temporary shelter, so much the better. You will save valuable money that otherwise would go into rent.
11. Learn as much as you can while you are "biding your time." Help others on building projects. I learned most of my skills by helping others.
12. Build everything you are capable of building. Rather than watch television; build your own cabinets, doors, shelves, furniture. This is good way to spend the winter nights when you are dreaming of your future home.

HOME OWNERS or FIRE INSURANCE

I have received numerous calls and emails asking how to get Homeowners or Fire Insurance on a cordwood home.

One key concept is to <u>call the home a masonry and wood home or simply a masonry home</u> rather than a cordwood home. Insurance agents don't have the word "cordwood" in their rate-books. But they do have masonry/wood homes. In fact cordwood homes usually get the same rate as stone or masonry homes.

The fire resistance tests from the University of New Brunswick (*Cordwood and the Code: A Building Permit Guide*) are invaluable in demonstrating to insurance agents that cordwood meets and exceeds the building and fire standards for single family dwellings.

10.3 Here comes the cordwood sun!

Cordwood Sheds & Pole Buildings

We started to run cordwood courses in 1984 and hit upon the idea of having the workshop participants get their hands "muddy" by working on an actual building. Since our house was finished, an outbuilding seemed like the way to go. We decided to use the pole building method.

10.4 The Cordwood Garden Shed at Treehaven (University of Wisconsin's Natural Resources Campus) near Tomahawk, WI.

We used pressure treated 4' x 4" posts (12' long) and buried them 4' in the ground. Then we made a "ladder pad" of pressure-treated 2" x 4"s turned on edge. The posts became the foundation and the framework for the walls and the support for the roof. So we framed the building up and had the course members mortar up a section or two, complete with their initials. By the time we had built four of these buildings we were putting on the roof ahead of time so we could mortar in the rain (and the shine). These buildings are an excellent way to practice your cordwood skills, work out your mistakes and have a functional, attractive building to boot. A person could build a doghouse, outhouse, garage, barn, playhouse, storage shed, etc. (We had one course family from Ohio that was going to erect these sheds as cabins, with a wooden floor, for a commercial wilderness camp they were building.) Take care to purchase supplies at sale prices and with a little bit of scrounging we put these 12' x 18' structures up (216 sq. ft.) for approximately a dollar a square foot. A set of full color plans titled *Cordwood Pole Shed Plans* is available in the ordering section at the end of this book.

10.5 Netonia Yalta's cordwood beauty on Haida Gwaii. BC

111

Cordwood Siding

(Faux cordwood can look so good)

This article is excerpted from Cordwood *Conference Papers 2005* by Richard Flatau.

10.6 Bob & Sheryl Gormley's patterned log-end workshop/store. The spinning wheel motif is made of 1.5" pieces of wood, glued and screwed onto a piece of painted, exterior plywood. (W. Marrier)

The Origin of Cordwood Siding

My cordwood home was complete and now my attention was drawn to building a greenhouse/solar room addition. (A greenhouse is almost a necessity for a committed gardener in Northern Wisconsin). My dilemma surfaced by way of a gentle hill that adjoined my home. The phone and electric wires were buried there and could not be moved to extend the foundation for the addition.

In order to obtain a suitable amount of space in the solar room, the "necessity is the mother of invention rule" reared its timely head. The solution became apparent as I began to stud out and "side" the exterior walls of the greenhouse/solar room with CDX plywood. I noticed a 2" cut-off piece of cedar log-end and held it up against the plywood. I wondered, "What if I glued and nailed log-end rounds like this and then mortared them in?" Chicken wire stapled to the plywood would hold the mortar nicely in place. With that problem out of the way I began cutting 1.5" pieces of cedar with my chain saw and placing them in random patterns on the CDX plywood. An interesting mosaic of cordwood rounds evolved and made the log end wall the focal point of the entrance to our home.

Cordwood Masonry Construction

Many people are drawn to the natural beauty of cordwood walls. The richly detailed log end surface coupled with a lightly colored mortar makes a subtle, attractive statement. Cordwood masonry construction (also known as Stackwall, Log-End or Stovewood) is a traditional building method of stacking 12"-24" log ends in a mortar matrix and insulating the middle cavity. This method of construction has stood the test of time. The R-factor for a well built cordwood home equals or surpasses that of a conventional stick-built home. The mortar matrix can be as simple as Portland cement and sand or as different as slurried newspaper, sand, hydrated lime and masonry mix. Cordwood can be the infilling within a timber framework or 30" long, 6" x 6" blocks can be used to make a stackwall corner. There are 100 year old barns and houses in Quebec, Wisconsin and Iowa. Cordwood masonry has experienced a modern revival of sorts over the last 30 years. Thousands of cordwood homes have been constructed in the US and Canada.

Where to Use Cordwood Siding

Natural builders long for the "look" of a cordwood wall, but oftentimes don't have the space or can't spend the time to "stack up" a cordwood wall. The way to get that cordwood look, without all the mortaring is to use cordwood siding.

There are a myriad of places & projects that lend themselves to cordwood siding:

- Gable ends
- Long runs of lumber over garage/exterior doors
- Additions
- Sheds
- Interior walls
- Doors

10.7 Cordwood log-ends glued and nailed to CDX plywood. 1" chicken wire is stapled to the plywood before the log-ends are attached and then a mortar mix is applied in stucco like fashion. (B. Flatau)

113

- Solar rooms
- Playhouse/tree house
- Ice fishing shanty
- Hunting cabins
- Headers over large windows & doors
- Doghouse/cathouse

The uses for cordwood siding are only limited by the imagination. When the sheer weight of a cordwood wall, mind-numbing time constraints or unfeasibility make it difficult to use full length cordwood on a project, why not consider using *cordwood siding* instead?

Chicken Coops and Cordwood Lodges

Tom Huber formerly of Watervliet, Michigan decided that a chicken coop he was refurbishing looked rather foul, dilapidated and uninviting. He decided to paint the OSB board a mortar white and then nailed and glued on log ends of various sizes and shapes. The result is a very attractive and "souped up" chicken coop that is pleasing to the eye. The chickens are reported to be laying more eggs in their newly refurbished digs.

10.8 This chicken coop had weathered OSB sheets before Tom Huber painted them and glued and screwed on 1.5" log ends. The chickens are reportedly cackling away in their refurbished "coop de ville." (T. Huber)

Emboldened by the success of the chicken coop, Tom then decided to refinish a wall of his cordwood/stone lodge. He painted a piece of 7/16" OSB board (he specifically used OSB to create a textured look) and then nailed 1.5" log ends to the plywood. The white paint simulates the mortar of a regular full length cordwood wall.

This cordwood sided wall is actually a 2" x 6"

10.9 This log end siding is 1.5" cedar and pine. The window trim and log ends are the same thickness & gives the wall a pleasant 3D effect. (T. Huber)

framed wall with 24" of stone veneer that is 8" thick at the base and gradually tapers to about 5" at the point where it meets the 1.5" cordwood log ends discs. The trim around the windows is the same thickness which helps tie in the log ends visually. The log ends were nailed into the OSB with two or three 2" brads (the kind used for hardwood trim). Tom did this so the log ends could easily be removed for any future changes. The posts on either side assist with creating the appearance of a true cordwood wall since they stand just proud of the face of the wall. Tom had a machinist friend slice his 1.5 inch log ends with a band saw, thereby providing a clean cut that dramatically exposed the grain of the wood.

The Art of Cordwood Siding

10.10 Bob constructed a handsome log-end design with a clever optical illusion on the side of the family's Starwood store. (B. Gormley)

Having already built his own 4,700 square foot cordwood home, Bob Gormley of Backus, Minnesota took the cordwood siding technique to a new level of artistry when he placed intricate, pre-planned patterns onto the CDX plywood of his workshop/store. I made it a point to call Bob when I saw pictures of his gorgeous homestead. The first question out of my mouth was, "How did you get the mortar joints so perfectly even?" He laughed politely and said, "Guess what Richard, there is no mortar." He painted the plywood with a durable, epoxy finish and then glued the log ends with construction adhesive and then secured them with torque head screws (through pre-drilled holes) from the inside of the plywood. Bob's wife, Sheryl is a spinner & weaver by trade, and so, he placed a spinning wheel on the side of their workshop/store (see picture at beginning of the article). Bob was able to plan ahead and make a template of his awesome creation.

Bob, like Emeril of TV Chef fame, "kicked it up a notch" with the side wall to his garage. He placed a well thought out visual/optical illusion on the street side of his workshop/store. As the picture shows, the illusion is one of the door being open and the unsuspecting passer by "sees" a view of the inside of the shop.

Using Cordwood Siding on the Interior

This log end siding technique could be very easily used on the INSIDE of an existing home. Sheets of ¼" to ½" plywood would be cut to fit a wall. The plywood would then be taken outside and painted with a durable interior paint. The log end sections would be glued and then screwed from the backside of the plywood. Then the whole piece would be moved to the room and attached to the studs. A few extra pieces would need to be added to break up the seams in the 4' x 8' sheets.

A couple of pointers would be in order to avoid problems.

1. The wood needs to be debarked and dry. It could even be "finished" for an interior room.

2. The paint needs to be of the highest quality (and non-toxic) because, needless to say, it needs to last for a long time. The newer textured paints might provide an interesting contrast.

3. The ideal way to secure the wood pieces is to glue them (with construction adhesive) and then screw them from the backside. If the wall cannot be reached from the backside, then the pieces would be screwed or nailed from the front, the nails/screws countersunk and covered.

4. "Slice and dicing" of the log ends can be accomplished with a chain saw (using a sawbuck to hold the log); a band saw (which would give a clean cut) and with smaller log ends a circular saw or table saw. No matter which method is used, safety is paramount and kickback is to be avoided at all costs. Wear safety glasses and be careful when using any power tools.

5. Pre-drill slightly smaller size holes prior to nailing or screwing the log ends, so that the 1.5 inch slices do not crack when securing them. In addition, pre-drill a smaller hole in the plywood to direct the backside "screw down" position of the log ends on the viewable side.

Pros & Cons of Cordwood Siding

When considering whether to go "full length' cordwood or simply cordwood siding, the "wood be" builder must ponder the following:

Pros **for constructing regular** *full length* **cordwood are:**

1. R-factor: 1" of cordwood equals an R-factor of 1.47. (24" wall ='s R-35).

2. The cordwood walls are the least expensive part of the building.

3. When the wall is mortared it is finished both inside and out.

4. The insulation is also completed.

Pros **for using** *cordwood siding***:**

1. Faster than regular cordwood.

2. If the wall is painted the walls go up quite quickly.

3. Provides for the cordwood "look" when regular length cordwood is not feasible.

Cons **for using** *cordwood siding*

1. The interior wall has to be insulated.

2. The interior wall has to be finished.

3. Not as durable as full length cordwood.

Cons **for using** *full length* **cordwood**

1. Time..

2. Labor intensive.

Next Time

The next time you are considering a building project and you want a "look" that is unique, warm and attractive, why not give cordwood siding the "once over?" You may be very pleased with your creation.

10.11 Flatau's metal garage with a cordwood siding face lift.

The Woodpile Tree

10.12 Some folks see a woodpile and think, "Oh a pile of wood," others see a woodpile and think "What beautiful creation can I make with this?"

Brilliant Bottles

10.13 The late Don Gerdes built a self contained bottle end box, which had a removable LED light. He could turn it on whenever he wanted to see color in his walls. He called his invention Brilliant Bottles.

Cordwood in the bathroom

10.14 Cordwood in the bathroom at Julie Dale's. The timber frame is recycled from a 150 year old warehouse in Janesville, Wisconsin. Cedar cordwood shelves at the edge of the tub and beautiful bottle ends for filtered light. (J. Dale)

I first met Clarke Snell, author of *Building Green*, when he came to speak at the Cordwood Workshop we held in Marshall, NC in 2007 at Love's Organic Farm and Permaculture School. He gave a brief talk and what he said made perfect sense. "House building is hard work and you had better be well prepared." He was one part charming, one part construction foreman, and one part prophet of doom.   A good combination when it comes to novices jumping into the Herculean task of homebuilding. He gives good advice to the "would be" owner/builder.   Listen carefully, if you want to be successful.

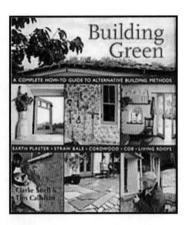

Cordwood in Perspective: My Two Cents Worth
by Clarke Snell

I live in a wooded mountainous area where lots of people heat their homes with wood. Around here, you can see huge piles of cordwood stacked like fortresses on the porches or in the yards of little, poorly insulated houses. A few months later, that wood is gone, burnt in a wood stove for winter heat. Herein lies the central allure of cordwood construction. If you heat with wood, those piles of neatly stacked firewood look a lot like walls already. Not only can you harvest a major building material from your own land, but you are *already* harvesting and storing it, only for another purpose

Cordwood Pros

If you live in the forest, then, the main advantage of cordwood is obvious: it's an abundant, locally available, affordable building material. If you choose to go with a cob mortar and sawdust insulation, you could collect almost all of your wall volume from your building site. That's saying something these days! In addition, laying cordwood requires only basic tools and simple skills. Once laid, cordwood walls require no additional finish such as drywall, plaster, or even paint. In the right hands, cordwood is beautiful, energy and resource efficient, and can be less expensive than other wall systems with similar performance.

Cordwood Cons

Cordwood construction takes a lot more forethought than other building techniques. In a world where the norm is to scribble a floor plan on an envelope as you dash down to the Home Depot to buy some 2x4's because you have to bang something together TODAY, it takes rare patience to cut and split wood and air-dry it under cover for at least a year before using it in a wall. In addition, the exposed end-grain of each piece of wood facing toward the exterior is susceptible to water infiltration and therefore mold, insects, and other damaging forces. For me, perhaps the main functional cordwood con is wood shrinkage which can cause gaps and cracks that lead to air infiltration and even separation of cordwood from the mortar.

118

Cordwood Performance

Comparing cordwood's thermal performance to a more conventional wall system is difficult to generalize and beyond the scope of this short summary. However, I will say that since cordwood is made on site, its thermal performance can be adjusted to suit the specifics of the house project it is serving. The thicker the wall, the better it will resist the flow of heat, so you can theoretically generate the performance you need by adjusting wall thickness. In colder climates, an option for increasing thermal performance is double wall cordwood masonry, a system employing two cordwood walls separated by a space filled with insulation. Wood is both a decent insulator and a good thermal mass, so it is competent at both resisting heat flow and holding heat. Another potential performance plus for cordwood is it's hygroscopic nature…it's ability to take on and give off water vapor in response to changes in humidity levels. This trait theoretically helps wood to balance indoor humidity levels and therefore potentially improve indoor air quality.

Cordwood Reality Check

House construction is hard work, and laying cordwood is no exception. If you are planning to do it yourself, be realistic about your physical capabilities. If you are planning to pay someone, realize that competent cordwood construction is a skill and requires quality control if a long-lasting energy efficient building is the goal. Mainly, remember that cordwood is only a portion of what goes into the construction of a finished habitable building. You still need a foundation, window and door framing, a roof system, heating and cooling strategies and systems, and all the other things that make a house much more complicated than most people realize. In fact, I recommend that you limit the cordwood portion of your building even further by installing cordwood as infill between a post and beam structure. This allows you to build a roof to work under, keeping your cordwood (and the infill insulation around it) dry through the construction process. For novice builders, a good option is to get a pro to build or help you build the post and beam structure and a roof, then do the cordwood infill yourself.

Cordwood: Yes or No?

To me a house is a complex animal. Every approach to construction has "pros" that can be exploited or squandered and "cons" that are most often just surmountable design challenges. Therefore, careful planning and good design followed through lovingly in the construction process are probably more important than materials choices. Given that, cordwood is without a doubt a wall infill to consider in many situations. My rule of thumb: If you've got enough wood around to burn it for heat, then why not build with it, too?

Check out the digital update on cordwood at www.thenauhaus.com Chapter 9.

Chapter 11   Photos & Conferences
Cordwood Photo Album

11.1   KimAnna Cellura-Shields masterpiece.   The Peace of Art Cafe in Del Norte, Colorado. A beautiful example of cordwood construction with bottle end art.

11.2 KimAnna's attractive Mermaid Cottage built within a post & beam framework.

Cordwood Photo Album

11.3 Alan Adolphsen of Maine used 14" aspen log ends to build his cordwood home. It is handsome, sturdy, and fits well into its surroundings. (A.Adolphsen)

11.4 Curt Hubatch & Annie Lyon of Wisconsin built this attractive guest house. It has six posts and six roof joists, six posts and an earthen roof. (Hubatch)

Cordwood Photo Album

11.5 Bracebridge Lodge. A Bed and Breakfast in Bracebridge, Ontario.

11.6 A cordwood cedar lodge in Port Angeles, Washington, built in 1929.

Cordwood Photo Album

11.7 A lovely cordwood, post and beam home in Rockmart, Georgia.

11.8 Bruce Lord's very attractive and well built, double-wall home in northern Alberta, Canada. (C.Shockey)

Cordwood Photo Album

11.9 Tom and Mary Barchacky built this beautiful garden cottage shed. It is made of mostly "repurposed" materials. (T. Barchacky) See the article on this garden shed in Backhome Magazine, #102 (September/October 2009). www.Backhomemagazine.com

11.10 This round cordwood home in Northern Wisconsin is built with 16" walls on a full basement. It has Permachink mortared on every interior and exterior wall surface to control air infiltration and log checking. It was built by a commercial log home company. (R. Flatau)

Cordwood Photo Album

11.11White Earth Reservation cordwood home. This home was built using a Native American mortaring crew, 16" white cedar and local development grants. The center cavity has closed cell foam insulation, the floor has radiant heat. (R. Flatau)

11.12 John Meilahn's handsome, cedar pumphouse/storage shed in northern Michigan. The cedar posts on the corners are cut on the two sides that will accept the cordwood and mortar. Note the attractive sunflower motif and the pumpkin face in the lower left hand corner. (W. Higgins)

Cordwood Photo Album

11.13 The Peter's built this lovely stackwall cordwood home in Copper Harbor, Michigan. It serves as a home and a business. Steve and John Meilahn run North Shore Builders. (W. Higgins)

11.14 A million dollar cordwood lodge in Wisconsin. Full basement, timber framed, designed by an architect, standing seam metal roof, three stories, 18" cedar walls. (R. Flatau)

Cordwood Photo Album

11.15   The Carlson's beautiful cordwood home near Rochester, NY (P. Turkow)

11.16 Peter Allemang's combination strawbale and cordwood home in Wiarton, Ontario. The bottom story is cordwood and the top story is cordwood & strawbale. Peter wrote about his project in the Cordwood Conference Papers. (P. Allemang)

Cordwood Photo Album

11.17 Jan & Joel Massie's cordwood sauna near Lake Superior. They built this as a family project after taking one of our cordwood workshops.

11.18 Marcy & Tom Melvig's gorgeous round, two storey cordwood home in the Upper Peninsula of Michigan. (Richard Flatau)

Cordwood Photo Album

11.19 Sam Felt's round, cypress home in Adel Georgia with arched doors and windows. Inspiration and picture courtesy of Jack Henstridge.

11.20 George & Paulette Beveridge's Camp Cordwood near Copper Harbor, Michigan. This is an internal bottle end wall. The blue bottles are in the shape of Michigan's Upper Peninsula. (R. Flatau)

Continental Cordwood Conferences
CoCoCo: An ongoing celebration

Once every five or six years a Cordwood Conference is held where cordwood builders meet to discuss fresh innovations and renew old friendships. The first one was held in 1994 in West Chazy, New York at the cordwood home of Rob & Jaki Roy, who were the inspiration for these events. Pompanuck Family Farm, Cambridge, New York hosted the 1999 gathering. At each conference Papers were written and presented, home tours were arranged, mortaring styles demonstrated and friendships cemented. The largest gathering, with 227 'CoCoCoNuts' was in 2005 in Merrill, Wisconsin, hosted by Richard & Becky Flatau. In June of 2011 the first Canadian Cordwood Conference, hosted by Dr. Kris Dick, was held at the University of Manitoba. This rich heritage is bound to continue as long as people are eager and willing to share their discoveries.

Continental Cordwood Conference 2011
June 11-12, 2011
University of Manitoba, Winnipeg, Canada

The Conference started with a three day cordwood workshop from June 8-10 at the Alternative Village at U of M. The Alternative Village was founded by the engineering department to establish a vehicle for research on renewable energy and alternative building materials.

A building framework was erected by the engineering graduate students. It was approximately 12' x 16' but because it contains many purposely engineered, whimsical irregular angles that is certainly not the actual square footage.

Dr. Kris Dick, Cliff Shockey and Richard & Becky Flatau served as instructors. 17 students came from the graduate engineering program and from around the world: Sweden, Iran, Honduras and from many parts of Canada. We called one group the 'Fab Five' who bonded and worked closely with one another to offer support and inspiration. One gentleman changed his whole building design during the workshop.

The building (which will be used as an Entrance Kiosk to the Alternative Village) is to be a model of research for cordwood. The strategy was to build and demonstrate as many different cordwood styles, mortars and types of wall as possible.
We tried:

- Hemp hurds (the waste produce of industrial hemp) in the mortar & insulative cavity
- Traditional sawdust mortar & sawdust insulation
- Cellulose mortar & cellulose insulation
- Double wall with hemp hurd mortar on the outside wall
- Cob and cordwood on the west section

Bottle ends were placed in the walls, along with stones, dimensional lumber and a metal bottle-end with the initials of each participant hand-stamped. Three days of building, discussion and conversation produced a cohesive team that enjoyed working and learning together.

The Cordwood Conference was coupled with the engineering department's annual Design Day Conference and in keeping with that tradition, the Saturday portion of the conference was an amalgamation of topics: strawbale, hempcrete, recycling, green roof, green energy and cordwood. Each registrant had an opportunity to sample three of the six formats. We then moved to the Alternative Village to see first hand the research that was taking place. Cordwood demonstrations were conducted with double wall and single wall mortars. We were also able to see the original U of M stackwall building from the mid-70's.

On Sunday we got down to the business of cordwood presentations from the Cordwood Conference Papers 2011. There was a video on slipforming with doublewall cordwood, presentations on cordwood in Sweden, special effects, Paper Enhanced Mortar, double wall + balewall, community constructed cordwood, a cordwood cottage garden shed, engineering perspectives, and lessons learned. *A special power point tribute was shown about the life of Jack Henstridge (the Grandfather of Cordwood), in whose memory the conference was held.*

The presentations were portions of the

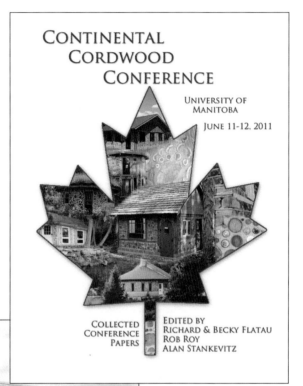

130 page *Cordwood Conference Papers 2011* which were given to each conference attendee. The Papers are the latest information in the ever evolving field of cordwood. (www.daycreek.com)

All things that have a beginning, have an ending, and the ending to this Conference was very magical, because

131

we were able to visit two cordwood/stackwall + balewall homes. Since we personally could only visit one home, we went to Clint and Cindy Cannon's double wall and balewall hybrid home. It was absolutely gorgeous. It brought the conference to a most harmonious conclusion since we journeyed during the five days, metaphorically, from cordwood construction theory, to hands-on building practice, to discussions of the various wall & mortar types; we witnessed impressive cordwood power point presentations and finally we arrived at the gestalt of being able to see the whole process in a beautifully constructed cordwood home.

In my humble opinion the marriage of double wall with balewall makes perfect sense on the cold, windy Canadian prairie.

Continental Cordwood Conference 2005

July 30-31, 2005
Merrill, Wisconsin

Drawn by Matt Taylor

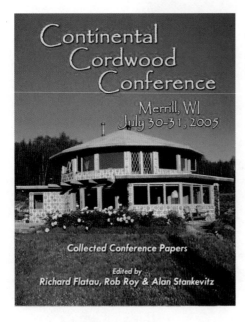

The Continental Cordwood Conference is a 126 page color document that contains 27 articles on "All Things Cordwood."

- Bright & Airy Cordwood homes
- Wraparound log ends
- Foam Insulation
- Paper Enhanced Mortar
- Lime Mortar
- Balewood (Strawbale & Cordwood)
- Frost Protected Shallow Foundations
- Octagonal Timber Framing
- Cordwood on a Basement
- Pattern Language and Cordwood
- Cordwood in Copper Country (MI)
- Cordwood Siding

- An Interview with Jack Henstridge
- Log Prep & Foam Insulation
- R-Value Testing from the U of Manitoba
- A Mortar Primer (Moving Mud)
- My Cordwood Dorm Room
- Engineer built home

Alan Stankevitz wrote a wonderful summary of the happenings at the Conference on his www.daycreek.com website. It is in the Journal under the title: *227 CoCoCoconuts*!

The Conference produced a booklet with a CD to deal with obtaining a building permit. The booklet, ***Cordwood and the Code: A Building Permit Guide*** is a 54 page document that contains:

- A summary of the cordwood method.
- The current testing on R-value from the Engineering Department of University of Manitoba.
- Current fire resistance testing from the Engineering Department University of New Brunswick.
- An explanation of the REScheck software from the US Department of Energy and a sample building permit application from Wisconsin using the REScheck software.

- A 17 page sample building permit document that was successful in obtaining a building permit.
- A transcript of a Conversation with a Code Official.

- A CD containing all of the stated information and the REScheck software, a copy of Adobe Acrobat reader 7.0, a read me file (explaining how to use the CD) and the 17 page sample building permit document, which can be cut and copied and pasted

Flatau's Chateau in Merrill. Wisconsin

to make your own building permit document that is applicable to your specific situation. This document will prove very useful in applying for and procuring a building permit.

White Earth Reservation Cordwood Home is a fine example of a **"Best Practices"** cordwood home. It is an important addition to the cordwood literature because we used closed cell foam insulation between the log ends like Sandy Clidaras demonstrated in his writings.

White Earth Reservation Cordwood Home   **Naytahwaush, Minnesota**
16" cedar cordwood infill, post and beam frame, 12:12 pitch room in the attic, foam insulation, radiant in-floor heat within an insulated sand bed.

Making Contact

In September of 2008 the MMCDC (Midwest Minnesota Community Development Corporation) contacted us with regard to the possibility of building a cordwood home on the White Earth Reservation in NW Minnesota. The idea was to provide attractive, affordable, energy efficient housing on the reservation, while offering employment opportunities for the training of tribal cordwood masons.

The plan to work with the White Earth Tribal Land Office allowed the home to be constructed on Tribal Trust Land. The local contractor and members of the tribe were enthusiastic about building a home that would be in harmony with the natural surroundings, be energy efficient and use locally available resources. It would be designed and built with wood from the area and in accord with Ojibwa home traditions. That is, the house would be a multi-generational home, it would incorporate a large family gathering area, the entrance would face east, and it would be comprised mostly of renewable materials. These factors were taken into account whenever possible. [Interviews were conducted with Ojibwa Tribal members in 2008 by Design Coalition of Madison, WI to explore different living space possibilities.] An architectural firm was hired to coordinate and include energy efficient and best practice construction methods with this home. Initial plans were drawn and after many discussions and consultations they were modified to meet the specific needs of the owner. Included in the plan was an energy 'heel' attic truss (which added 800 sq. ft. of living space as upstairs rooms). The plans produced a three bedroom, two bath, 1840 sq. ft. home. A large kitchen, dining, living area with an 'open concept' was incorporated in the final floor plan.

Vision

This article will undertake to describe the processes and unique attributes of this very successful home building project. They are:

- Efficient design with owner input (Ojibwa Tribal Member) leading to functional space usage
- 12/12 pitch roof for additional 800 sq. ft. adding 2 bedrooms, and a bath upstairs
- Insulated sand bed with radiant-in-floor heat (coupled with off-peak power usage)
- Northern White Cedar post and beam framework (a sacred tree in Ojibwa culture)
- 16" Northern White Cedar cordwood log ends
- High R-value foam insulation in center cavity (R-30)
- Cold weather mortaring techniques
- Ojibwa design features mortared into the cordwood walls
- Ojibwa mortaring crews hired

Good People

We were fortunate to work with two very capable builders: Robert Zahorski, the general contractor and Bill Paulson, a tribal member who was the project coordinator. Each dovetailed into the other's strengths and the result was a building that evokes Ojibwa traditions, built with 21st century construction techniques.

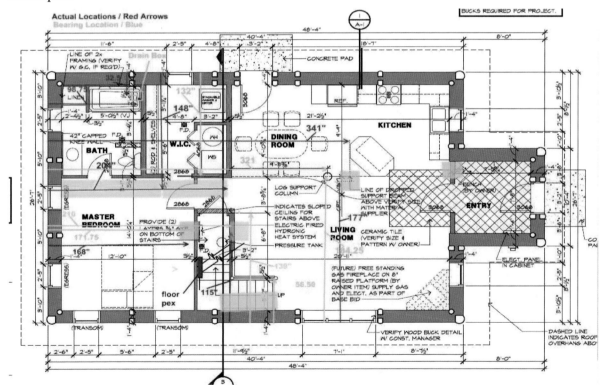

Final floor plan for 1840 sq. ft. home (1,040 sq. ft. first floor, 800 sq. ft. second floor.)

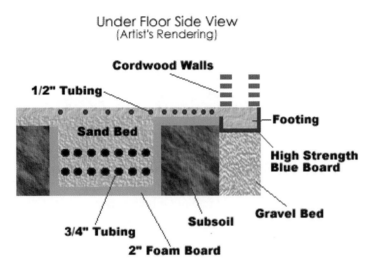

Under Floor Side View
(Artist's Rendering)

Cordwood Walls

1/2" Tubing

Footing

Sand Bed

High Strength
Blue Board

Gravel Bed

Subsoil

3/4" Tubing

2" Foam Board

Sand bed for heat storage

In the fall of 2009 the foundation was built with an insulated sand bed, beneath an insulated cement slab. This sand bed will store heat during off-peak energy hours and then radiate it throughout the house during the high-energy-rate use daylight hours. This is similar to radiant-in-floor heat, except the large sand bed under the foundation is insulated and provides heat energy storage for the home. The drawing on the left, courtesy of Alan Stankevitz of daycreek.com, gives a rendering of this concept.

Cedar post and beam framework

The post and beam framework was erected by a local contractor. Cedar posts gathered from near the reservation were milled on the two sides that would abut the cordwood infill. They were left rounded on the interior and exterior.

After the foundation was complete, the framework was built. In the adjoining picture, the cedar post and beam framework is erected and braced. The bracing is very important to maintain structural integrity and prevent sections from going out of square. The braces are only removed after the cordwood walls approach the four foot mark. As you will notice, the roof is complete and shingled. Having the roof finished before cordwood construction begins means that the cordwood mortaring can take place, for the most part, out of the elements. If a section is not finished in time, it can be 'boarded up' for the winter and work can continue on the inside of the building. Attaching tarps to the fascia boards is helpful when it is necessary to protect the mortar and the workers from the drying rays of the sun.

Electrical

There are many code compliant ways to run electrical wiring in a cordwood building. In general for wiring jobs we recommend that you follow your local building codes. In cordwood buildings in various parts of the country, we have used conduit, Romex NM, and UL 12-2 wiring (with a resistant coated jacket) wire-stapled to the middle of the posts. In this particular instance the electrical contractor chose to run flexible, plastic tubes (also called flexible PVC conduit). In accord with the blueprint, the 'blue smurf' wiring tubes were then installed throughout the building. The hanging blue tubes (with metal receptacles) were very irritating to work around during construction. The masons were constantly bumping into them while mortaring.

Window Boxes

The window boxes (made of double 2" x 8"s) were hung, using the sturdy top plates as fastening points. The two exterior door frames were 'roughed in.' Later these would have doors with beautiful etched glass panels installed for both privacy and beauty (see picture at end of article).

The window boxes, door framing and wiring tubes are shown in the accompanying photo. Notice that the window boxes are screwed into the top plate of the post and beam framework. This helps to assure that the windows will always open.

Cedar Log Ends

Early in the process, the decision was made to use 16" cedar log ends for the cordwood infill. This length would provide an insulation value of R-24. The logs had been cut and dried for four years in eight foot lengths. After that they were cut into 16" lengths and 70% of the logs were split to assure faster drying.

On the way to being stacked the logs were dipped in a borate solution (four cups of borax to one gallon of water). Finally, the logs were stacked in single rows for drying. While stacked, the exterior ends of the log ends were brushed with a UV blocker (Lifeline Exterior from Permachink) so that the faces of the exterior log ends would maintain their color. The interior log end faces were left natural.

Mortar Mixing

A mortar mixer was purchased and three different individuals were trained on mixing proper cordwood "mud." It was very helpful to have an alternate "mortar mixer" when someone had a scheduling conflict.

The mortar mixture used was the *Flatau's favorite mix* of:

- 1 part Portland Cement
- 1 part Hydrated Lime Type S
- 2 parts soaked softwood sawdust (coarse)
- 3 parts washed, coarse sand

The overall feel of the mortar is an adobe style texture which is easily tuck-pointed with a spoon.

Injecting Foam Insulation

For insulation, the initial strategy was to use regular coarse softwood sawdust mixed with hydrated lime in the center cavity, but a dearth of coarse, softwood sawdust in the area, led to another decision. It was determined that injected closed cell foam was going to be used. The main advantages of injected foam are: high R-value (R-7 per inch), it bonds well with the wood and tends to fill every nook and cranny. Cordwood builder Sandy Clidaras of Quebec has been a pioneer in using closed cell foam in single wall cordwood and so we consulted him for advice. Sandy generously gave of his time and information. Convinced of the foam's merits, we ordered eight kits of foam insulation.

When using injected closed cell foam the cordwood wall is first built in two-foot-high sections. Half-inch tubes are inserted in the center cavity as the wall is being built. The mortar is left to harden for at least 24 hours (any sooner and the wall may be lifted by the pressure of the expanding foam). The foam is then injected into the tubes. The foam comes in two canisters, which must be warmed before being used and then shaken while injecting (this makes certain all the foam is used). There are many companies that make expanding foam and quite a number of building supply stores carry the kits. To find a foam retailer, do a Google search and make a few phone calls to get your best price. On a

1,200 square foot home, with eight foot high cordwood walls, the foam will add approximately $4000 to the cost of construction.

[Note: See article in these papers by Sandy Clidaras: *Foam Insulation,* for further details on how much foam to order and some of his special injecting instructions. Always wear recommended protective gear when using foam.]

The closed cell foam is rated at an R-value of 7 per inch. A 5 inch cavity gives an R-value of 35. Coupled with the usual 16" cordwood walls' R-value of R-24, we extrapolated that our wall R-value approached R-30.

Bill Paulson (right) devised an ingenious method of making sure foam got in every crack and crevice.. He was the 'main-man foamer' and if he detected a cavity was not completely filled he would drill a hole in the longitudinal middle of a log end , place a 3/8" pex tubing hose into the log end until it reached the bottom and then inject foam into the unfilled cavity. Bill developed a method of slowly pulling out the

tube, as he injected the foam (one hand on the nozzle trigger and one hand on the tube). He became quite accomplished at stopping the flow of the foam before it erupted over the top. It was helpful to have a "foam watcher" telling the "foamer" how close the expanding foam was to the top. After completion of the home, an infrared scan showed no 'cold spots' in the cordwood walls.

Cold Weather Mortaring

When we left to conduct another workshop in North Carolina the cordwood mortaring crew was about one third finished. Little did we know at the time that the fall of 2009 in northwestern Minnesota would turn into one of the coldest on record. Finishing the cordwood infill in October meant tarping the house, covering the cordwood walls with blankets and 'firing-up' a propane heater. Starting a little later in the morning allowed the temperatures to rise a bit.

If at all possible, cold weather mortaring is something to avoid. If the water in the mortar mix freezes it can cause the mortar to flake and crumble. Since this home was built within a post and beam framework there was no worry about structural integrity, but to have to re-mortar a complete wall or part of a wall would become a very labor intensive operation, especially since the mortar flaking may not be immediately apparent.

If you must mortar in cold weather, it is imperative to finish all mortaring before freezing temperatures occur. If this becomes impossible, then precautions need to be taken to assure the mortar will not freeze:

- The freshly mortared cordwood wall must be covered with blankets or tarps and secured, so it is protected from freezing cold and wind.

- If there is a crew working on different sections (as was the case on this project) wrap the entire building with tarps to cover the work. (see picture)
- Even though there is a little heat generated from the chemical reaction of the Portland cement and the water, it is not enough to prevent it from freezing when the temperatures plummet.
- On this project, not only did we tarp the entire house, but we placed a propane heater in the middle of the house to keep the mortar from freezing.
- It is very important to keep the walls covered, except when mortaring, for at least seven days.
- According to masonry experts, masonry mortar takes seven days to dry and fourteen days to cure.

There are ingredients that can be added to the mortar mix to retard freezing (calcium chloride), but with the soaked sawdust in this mix, no one can adequately be certain that these non-freeze agents will work properly. So it is best to cover, seal and provide a source of heat if the temperature is going into the 20's. Diminishing the amount of sawdust as temperatures drop can be helpful, as the retarding feature of

the sawdust is less important.

On this project we were properly prepared to prevent the masonry from freezing during the very cold month of October 2009. While the precautions kept the cordwood walls from freezing, it added to labor costs by requiring time consuming 'take-down' every morning and 'button-up' in the evening. The cordwood masonry was finished by late October and the inside work commenced. The entire cordwood infill was accomplished in less than six weeks.

Native Cordwood Masons

One of the highlights of this project was meeting and teaching the cordwood mortaring group which had been assembled for this task. The crew was paid a good wage and learned valuable masonry and construction skills in the process. They were enthusiastic and learned quickly. As the project went along, some of the guys started talking about building an Ojibwa Ceremonial Lodge and personal homes, using the abundant Tamarack on the edges of the surrounding wild rice lakes. One of the many side benefits of being involved in this project was receiving gifts of hand harvested and processed wild rice. Even though the project was open to women applicants, there were no takers. Becky ended up being the only woman on the crew and enjoyed working with the guys.

The Ojibwa medicine wheel is prominently displayed on the front room wall. The colors and placement all have symbolic value.

Special Effects

Bill and Robert were instrumental in making some of the artistic Ojibwa motifs in the White Earth

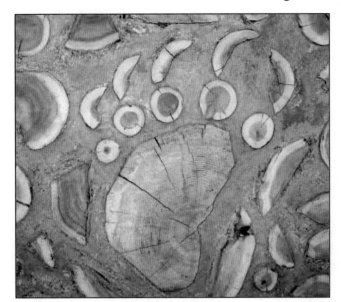

Home. The owner of the home was a member of the Bear Clan, so Bill decided he would put a bear paw in the cordwood wall. It became one of the focal points of the house.

The feather blends attractively into the entrance wall. The cordwood home has been occupied for many years and the owner, a school teacher on the reservation, raves about the naturally beautiful cordwood home.

We visited the home a year after completion to do any weatherizing that might be required We applied Permachinktm around a few log ends that had loosened and stuffed a few round log ends that had checked with white fiberglass. This well constructed home is easy to heat and blends beautifully into the surrounding woodland.

The home has caused quite a stir in the surrounding area, and there are plans for building a commercial law office, a ceremonial lodge and more cordwood homes. We are proud of our involvement, and grateful for the friendships made, but we are also thankful to the tribal members who welcomed us and provided insight and assistance in making this home come to fruition. Being involved in a project of this magnitude was certainly a peak experience for us.

Addendum 2

> The article below first appeared in the Mother Earth News in 1984 and brought notoriety to our homestead. We had visitors from all 50 states before the hoopla died down. That article fostered many workshops, three books, TV & radio appearances and subsequently the facilitating of the very successful Cordwood Conferences in 2005 and 2011. The turmoil and blessings that may come with undertaking a major life decision, like home building, still resonate.

Our Mortgage Free Cordwood Castle

Preface

The following selection is my personal narrative, written for *The Mother Earth News* that recaptures the construction of my own cordwood abode. It is meant to serve as an introduction to the main body of material that follows and hopefully will alert the reader to the current trends and changes in cordwood building. It is entitled: **"Our Mortgage Free Cordwood Castle."** It still rings true, many years later.

Getting Started

The notorious winter of 1978 left me with an empty oil tank, a barren pocketbook, wood choppers back and a mind whirling with fresh fantasies of building my own home. One -20° below zero night in January, while burning the midnight oil and pouring over a growing pile of "How-to-Build" books, I happened upon an article describing cordwood

Hearthstone Soapstone Wood Stove (750 pounds, heats 2,000 sq.ft.)

masonry construction. The crisp, beautiful color photos enticed me and the ensuing narrative whetted my imagination with its low cost, owner built, sweat equity appeal. Cordwood construction was, most definitely worthy of further serious investigation.

Discovery

Having perused and priced log and conventional homes, stone structures, rammed earth abodes, pole buildings, geodesic domes, foam domes, earth sheltered homes, active and passive solar homes, it became clear that none of these methods would allow the realization of my dream of a mortgage free, owner built home. My financial plan "costed out" at $5,000 to erect the shell and $15,000 for the finished product; with the capital coming from savings, life insurance policies, bi-weekly paychecks and equity from the sale of our mortgaged home.

The cordwood construction article was packed with dollar facts on three different structures: One built in New Brunswick, Canada, for $10,000 (3,000 sq. ft.), another in Upstate New York for $6,000 (1,000 sq. ft.), and a water tank storage building with 24" thick walls near Calgary, Alberta, for $4,000 (1,500 sq. ft.).

Cordwood masonry construction, for the uninitiated, is a method of building walls by stacking lengths of wood (12" to 24"), as one would erect a stack of firewood. A 3" inch mortar-cement mixture is placed on the outside and inside, one row at a time, and the center is insulated. The finished product looks rather like a stone wall.

Decision Making

Making a final decision required purchasing or borrowing the three available books on cordwood construction. Jack Henstridge sent his humorously written *Building the Cordwood Home* , complete with an energetic, enthusiastic, encouraging note answering various queries, Rob Roy's book, *How to Build Log-End Houses*, was obtained through the Wisconsin inter-library loan system and provided valuable information on mortar mixes, mortaring techniques, drying times, patience and potential pitfalls. The University of Manitoba's book, *Stackwall: How to Build It*, written by their civil engineering staff, contained concise formulas for determining exact amounts of wood, sand, cement, mortar, lime, etc., per sq. ft. of wall; along with a unique railroad tie, gravel berm-foundation plan which they utilize effectively in their "Low Cost Housing for the North" projects. The University of Manitoba also offers courses in the actual "hands on" construction of a cordwood building.

Preparation

After reading and rereading each book, the decision was "Go" for a cordwood house, if enough cedar (14 cords) could be obtained. That proved little enough trouble here in northern Wisconsin. A "want-ad" in the local newspaper and a phone call to the DNR forest ranger led the way to procuring 14 full cords of cedar. Cedar is the ideal (though not the only) wood for cordwood construction use, since it provides a light, pleasant appearance, has a refreshing fragrance, offers fine insulating qualities (1.25 R per inch), and is naturally decay resistant. Most any softwood can be used: pine, tamarack, larch, balsam, hemlock, or any other low density wood is acceptable. The most important point to remember is that whatever wood one chooses, it must be: BARKED, DRIED and SPLIT so that shrinkage between mortar and wood is kept to a minimum. Hour upon hour was spent with ruler, protractor, pencil, eraser, and graph paper designing the interior and exterior. It is infinitely simpler to move a wall, room, cabinet, plumbing fixture, electrical outlet, or door on graph paper rather than after it is firmly in place. My wife thought my hand had sprouted a measuring tape appendage, as I was continually marking off and measuring imagined rooms, doors, and closets.

Materials

The cedar was purchased for $350, or approximately $28 a cord. The cement and mortar ran $140, 11 yards of sand $35, and 40 bags of hydrated lime $80, including innumerable free loads of sawdust from a local sawmill. The total exterior and interior wall cost for the entire house was $505 (9,600 cubic feet); a considerable savings over the conventional stud wall.

The posts and beams were selected from the straightest and soundest cedar logs and squared on two sides at a local sawmill. These were placed on a pressure treated 2" x 12" framework which had been anchor bolted to the 30' x 40' insulated, "floating" slab. The top plate was a double 2" x

10" that effectively tied the post and beam framework together. Door and window openings were framed and squared with 2" x 10"s. Electrical boxes and wires were positioned on all walls with conduit and/or UF wire as the building codes allowed.

Laying Up a Wall

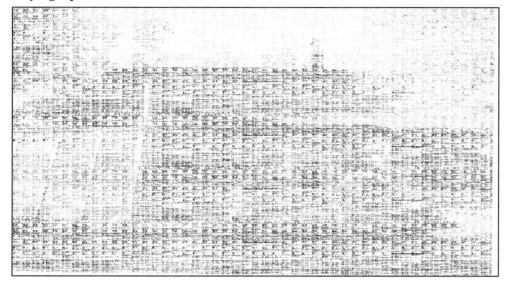

Flatau's Chateau in the fall with pumpkins from the garden on the deck.

With the post and beam framework in place the walls were ready to be "mudded up". Choosing the correct mortar mix is perhaps the most critical phase of cordwood construction. The proper combination of sand, Portland cement, water, hydrated lime, and damp sawdust is crucial; it was Rob Roy who suggested using soaked sawdust to improve the insulating qualities of the wall and make the mortar "set" better. As with all "wood masons" a "just so" mixture evolves. Mine consisted of: 3 parts fine sand, 1 part Portland cement, 1 part hydrated lime, 3 parts damp sawdust and enough water to make a very thick, workable "mud". This time tested ratio looks nice (an off-white color), sets up slowly (a masonry plus), holds a tight bond around the wood, and provides an extra insulative barrier against the cold.

My 12.5" cedar logs were set in, one row at a time, (other builders have used from 8" to 24" logs), mortar placed on the inside and outside 3" and an insulating sawdust/lime mixture laid down the middle. The post and beam framework proved incredibly handy since I only needed to work on one 8' square section at a time. Two people working with a cement mixer could put up one full section in 8-10 hours time. As the walls rose the structure took on a stone fortress-like effect and visitors began rolling in to gawk, talk, and sometimes even work. The ubiquitous sidewalk superintendents that wandered through quickly fell into two categories: those "prophets of doom" who raved that cordwood construction was virtually impossible since they had never seen it before, and those few encouraging visionaries who delighted in the innovative style, simple lines, native materials and owner built motif.

We were always looking to contain costs. For example, the trusses, with a room built in, were made at a local truss plant for $800 less than the cost of a conventional "stick-built" roof. These room-in-the-trusses provided an extra 560 sq. ft. of living space that now includes 2 bedrooms, a play area, ample storage and a half bath. After putting up the trusses, rainstorm followed rainstorm as we struggled to sheath and shingle the roof. On August18 the house was finally and happily covered. After breathing a deep sigh of relief the windows and doors were placed in their previously framed openings.

Thus, our cordwood castle was "shelled" and ready for the winter of 1979-1980 at a cost of $4,755. Work continued during the winter as the upstairs floor (1/2" plywood under 5/8" particle board) and stairs were completed and the first floor rooms studded out.

Decisions, Decisions

With the ensuing spring came a difficult decision. 1980 saw skyrocketing inflation, a Presidential Election (Carter vs. Reagan), hostages in Iran and interest rates at an all time high (20%). We were attempting to sell our house in town, use the equity to finish the cordwood home, and move out to our "back forty". Buyers were scarce as hen's teeth, so we borrowed $8,000, to be paid back as soon as the house sold. Interior work accelerated to a fever pitch with this newly acquired capital. The water pump was placed into the existing refurbished well, plumbing lines and fixtures installed, cabinets mounted, Norway Pine ceilings and walls erected, closets, built-in bookcases, pantry and work tables completed.   (We had inished our cordwood home for just under $15,000 in 1980 dollars. It was our goal and our dream to become mortgage-free and now we were!)

Emotional Strain

Perhaps the most pervasive emotion that manifested itself the last year of building was Anxiety. What if the housing market didn't improve? Could we leave the country house unheated if we didn't sell the city house? Would we be able to make the mortgage payments and continue construction on the cordwood home? Being a strong-willed sort, I had no qualms about tackling the physical, mental and spiritual aspects of building a domicile; but the emotional stress of being helpless to affect the larger economic picture was frightening.

As fate would have it (spurred on with blood, sweat, prayers and tears) the city house sold in October. Debts, bills and I.O.U.'s were paid immediately and a small sum was left over for the savings account. On October 10, we spent the first night in our mortgage free, cordwood "castle" and have drunk in its subtle cedar scent and fetchingly simple beauty ever since. Nestled in the front-center of 40 acres of glaciated hardwood and pine forest it is, most assuredly a gladsome sight on my daily trek home from work.

*Richard, Becky & Summer
on a warm spring day.*

*This article is still on the Mother Earth News website.   www.motherearthnews.com
There are more and different pictures than are shown here.*

CORDWOOD CABIN
BEST PRACTICES

RICHARD & BECKY FLATAU

ENERGY EFFICIENT DESIGN

RENEWABLE RESOURCES

Addendum 3

(A condensed version of Cordwood Cabin for Cordwood Construction: Best Practices)

The following pages demonstrate how we built a 'best practices' cordwood building for our local school district.   This is a condensed version of the book *Cordwood Cabin* (by Richard & Becky Flatau).   This booklet is included in *Cordwood Construction: Best Practices* to give the reader an example of one way to build a 'best practices' state-of-the-art cordwood cabin.

This addendum contains all of the following information:

- planning
- drawing (detailed plans, blueprints)
- code compliance
- wood harvesting and drying
- foundation (Frank Lloyd Wright rubble trench/frost protected shallow foundation (FPSF)
- framing
- window boxes
- door framing
- electrical
- energy heel (high heel) trusses
- mortar mixes
- cordwood mortaring and tuck pointing
- special effects in the walls
- solar thermal panels and PV panels
- fund raising for community projects
- using community volunteers effectively
- book and literature list
- links and websites

We were blessed with a beautiful building site (on the 764 acre Merrill School Forest), an excellent, committed group of volunteers, sustainable timber harvesting, a "green" focus and a determined set of leaders to see the project through to completion.

It is our hope that you can pick and choose which of the following best practices works for your project.   Cordwood construction is an ever evolving field and we welcome your insights, innovations and ideas.

Cordwood Cabin

Building the Cordwood Education Center

Using Best Practices & Energy Star™ Guidelines

Richard & Becky Flatau

© 2012

Cordwood Construction Resources LLC

Merrill, WI

The Cordwood Center with its blanket of winter snow

"A house built of logs will be like none other, for it will glorify the stick."
-Frank Lloyd Wright

Foreword

by Rob Roy

With a fresh copy of this new book in hand, Richard and Becky showed up at our Earthwood booth at the 2009 Midwest Renewable Energy Fair. I had a quick look at it and knew immediately that it was a carefully crafted document. I flipped page after page, impressed by the wealth of information and detail. Two days later, I had the opportunity to hear the authors deliver a 50-minute illustrated lecture on the same subject, the creation of the Cordwood Education Center in the woods near Merrill, Wisconsin. It was as thorough and well-prepared as the book. A year earlier, my wife, Jaki, and I had had the opportunity to actually visit the building in progress and we could see in a trice that, indeed, all the i's were dotted and the t's crossed. The place fairly reeked of quality, careful planning and "best practices" building techniques.

Finally, two weeks after the Fair, I had the time to read the entire document, only to discover that the book was even more thorough than I had expected. This concise work crams an awful lot into its 60-odd pages: valuable information on the rubble trench foundation, the timber framing, the cordwood masonry, and so many other building techniques appropriate to this structure as well as others. And, while the Cordwood Center is primarily used for educational purposes, the lessons learned - and clearly taught herein - are appropriate for a bright, beautiful energy efficient home, just as the authors intended.

But Rich and Becky also set out to show other groups how they, too, could accomplish a community project like this one … or even one which is completely different! Follow the little yellow lightning bolts throughout the book and you will score a myriad of practical tips about how to successfully organize almost any kind of community project.

Once again, the Flatau's show why they are respected leaders in the cordwood field, and I don't just say this because they let us sleep in the Spare Bedroom where they publish (and continually update) their several works. I really mean it.

Rob Roy is Director of Earthwood Building School in West Chazy, New York, which, with his wife Jaki, he has operated since 1981. He has authored some 15 books in the alternative building field, including several on cordwood masonry.

Purpose

This book is being written for a number of reasons. The first one is to *provide a model from which "best practices" homes, cottages and cabins can be built.* This project could be modified to be a full sized lodge or a small cabin. The plans are architecturally drawn and it would be fairly simple to increase or decrease the length and width in 4 to 8 foot sections.

The second reason for writing this tome is to not only *document the process, but also to honor all of those who participated in this "most excellent" community building project.* This is most certainly a testament to the enabling power of positive energy.

The third reason that is becoming much clearer as the building gets more and more attention, is *to develop an outline by which groups can successfully complete a similar project.* To that end, the basic framework could be "infilled" with any number of alternative techniques. The infill in the walls could be strawbale, cob, light straw-clay, SIPS, earth blocks, or vertical log siding. The idea herein, is to provide a model of a building that could be modified to meet a group's specific plan. If this were built in the desert southwest, cob or adobe might be the better choice. On the plains, where straw is more plentiful than wood, strawbale could be the answer. The infill is a choice made by natural surroundings and community resources.

> **"If you can dream it, you can do it."**

Introduction

This is the story of the journey to erect a community built, privately funded cordwood shelter for a local school system. This beautiful shelter was built on school forest land, in the heart of the Wisconsin north woods. The mighty Wisconsin River flows nearby and is complemented by one of the most diverse terrains in the state. The Ice Age Trail runs adjacent to the site, so the topography is glaciated land sculpted 10,000 years ago by a mile high ice sheet. The forest is second and third growth timber and is predominately pine, aspen, maple, and tamarack with significant undergrowth.

The building of the Cordwood Education Center is a story of unbridled enthusiasm, dedicated volunteers, intelligent pre-planning and hours of work.

Built off grid, the site had to have a generator for power, a 250 gallon water tank for water, and the always important "porta-potty."

Topics

This book will discuss the following ideas.

There will be a consideration that runs throughout this book which deals with how the project was successfully completed, by taking into account how the three committees functioned and made decisions. Cordwood harvesting and preparation will be reviewed. Frank Lloyd Wright's rubble trench foundation and how it was utilized on this project will be explained. Looking at tasks that may be completed during winter is instrumental in lessening the workload during the building season. Effective and safe post and beam framing, a primer on cordwood masonry and examples of "Best Practices" that were incorporated into this structure, will be discussed. Also included is a materials list, a recommended reading list and record of valuable websites and blogs dealing with cordwood and related topics. The renewable energy component is still in the process of being investigated, 'costed,' and built. Suggestions on how and where to get the latest information on renewable energy instruction is included.

 Community & Group Suggestion Boxes

Throughout this book there will be suggestions for groups who want to attempt a similar project. There is, in addition, a chapter at the end entitled: **Go Forth and Do Likewise**.

The group suggestions will be marked with a yellow lightning bolt.

Table of Contents

Chapter 1

Pre-Planning

One of the most difficult and most important aspects of building is to get all one's "ducks in a row." Rushing headlong into a project can often result in a poorly built structure that requires many "do-overs." This Cordwood Center is a testament to proper pre-planning and "proper alignment of ducks."

In the early winter of 2006, the School Forest Director at the Merrill School Forest asked us if we would make a presentation to the School Forest Advisory Committee about the possibility of building a Cordwood Warming House. The Warming House would be located approximately a mile away from the main lodge on a good gravel road and it would overlook a 10 acre beaver marsh. It would be a place for the students to get warm on their daily hike.

We made a power point presentation which consisted of detailing the best practices currently being used with cordwood construction. In addition, since all the members of the committee were committed to making the building as energy efficient as possible, it was decided that every effort would be made to ensure that this building was as "green, sustainable, and renewable" as possible. In fact one of the evolving goals was to make it into an example of alternative construction and renewable energy.

In a subsequent meeting, the Assistant Superintendent of Schools suggested that we have the plans for the building architecturally drawn and state code approved, before being presented to the School Board of Education for approval. This "charge" gave us an opportunity to spend time with an architect, designing the building to utilize best practices with cordwood while incorporating energy efficient building techniques.

 Create an attractive power point to inform the community.

 Do everything possible to dot all the i's and cross all the t's.
Being pro-active, with realistic expectations is a key factor in keeping the momentum going.

Disclaimer
The authors of this book have given an honest, straight-forward accounting of building a cordwood cabin. Since there are many factors which affect building a cordwood cabin: climate, water properties, mortar mixes, indigenous wood species, etc., the authors disclaim any and all responsibility for problems which may arise during and after construction.

Architectural Design

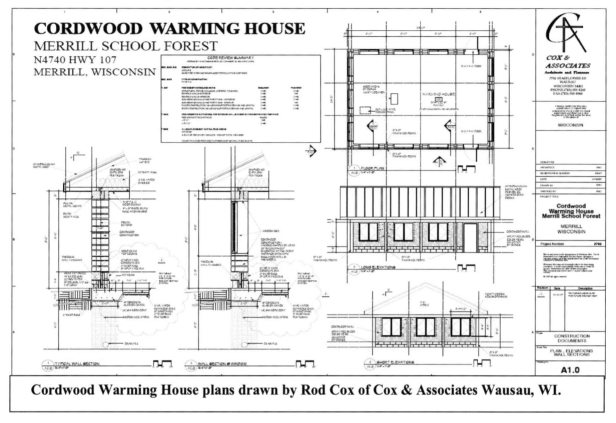

Cordwood Warming House plans drawn by Rod Cox of Cox & Associates Wausau, WI.

Many of the design features of the building became solidified after a visit to the Aldo Leopold Legacy Center in Baraboo, WI. The Aldo Leopold Legacy Center is a private foundation that uses its LEED certification (Leadership in Environmental Energy Design) to inspire and encourage others to "go forth and do likewise." www.aldoleopold.org.

A side trip to the "greenest public building in the state," the Mead Wildlife Visitors Center also inspired us through its renewable energy and sustainable design features. The Mead Wildlife Center is "Green by Design" and incorporates wind, photovoltaic, solar hot water, geothermal and biomass. Not only is it 73% more efficient than a regular code building, but it is also a very attractive building. www.meadwildlife.org Since this project was for a school district facility, the staff member who handles the Solar Wise Program (Wisconsin Public Service's program to educate high school students about renewable energy) was brought on board to assist in developing a photovoltaic/electricity element and solar in-floor radiant heat component. A master electrician volunteered to assist in the planning and execution of the solar design. The master electrician was part of a larger strategy to encourage community professionals to participate in the planning, design and construction of the building.

The State of Wisconsin, Department of Buildings and Safety, code approved the building the following spring. The Board of Education approved the building later that year.

Asking building professionals to help with the project is a way of ensuring quality workmanship and at the same developing ownership of the project within the community.

Chapter 2

Cordwood Harvesting: Peeling, cutting and splitting

Endeavoring to use sustainably-harvested materials, a local logger was hired to cut 25 cords of tamarack adjacent to the building site. The wood was cut and piled in preparation for peeling. It is common wisdom that wood cut in the spring is easier to peel because the sap is rising. Using that information the wood was peeled in the spring. Wood for cordwood needs to season for approximately 1.5 years to be fully dry for use in a cordwood wall.

2.1 Twenty-five cords of Tamarack, half-peeled and waiting for the mosquitoes to subside, so the crews can return.

2.2 Community volunteers put their 'heart & soul' and backs into the work.

Shovels, peeling spuds, ice scrapers, bent necked hoes and draw shaves were all used to peel the tamarack logs. Many adults found it took 15 minutes to a half hour to peel one eight foot "stick."

2.3 An ice scraper, a cut off shovel, a draw shave, a straightened hoe and a log carrier.

The students from the schools who were having their 'day' at the school forest lent a hand with the peeling. Working in teams they managed to peel many of the logs that are now part of the building. Groups of young men from Rawhide (a private juvenile rehabilitation facility, founded by Green Bay Packer Bart Starr) came to work on the logs and proved to be very competent peelers.

Plan to have at least 4 to 12 volunteers for peeling, cutting and stacking the cordwood. This is one of the more labor intensive jobs with cordwood.

The peeled wood was then cut into 16" lengths with a buzz saw. These were then split into various shapes (halves, thirds, fourths, fifths, and random designs). The reason for splitting log ends is to help them dry more thoroughly and reduce log loosening and checking. The more random and varied the log end splits the better the "look" of the finished cordwood walls.

2.4 Cutting wood to length with a buzz saw. The green stake is a 16" cut off guide.

Approximately 30% of the 16" lengths were left round. Round pieces give an enhanced appearance to the wall. The larger round pieces were taken inside to dry. The primary "check" that develops in a round piece was then stuffed with white fiberglass to stop air infiltration.

2.5 Using a mechanical splitter saves time.

The wood was stacked in long ricks or rows. The rows had lumber underneath to keep the log ends off the ground. Metal stakes were driven into the ground to support the ends, so that the logs could be stacked "up to" 5 feet high. The rows of wood were then covered on top, so that air and sun could dry the log ends and rain and snow would be kept off the top. The best row orientation is north to south. This is so that the wood is exposed to the morning sun from the east and the afternoon sun from the west.

Log ends used for cordwood construction need to be air dried to approximately 12% moisture content, according to the *Forest Products Wood Handbook*. A low moisture content is critical to avoid log ends loosening in the mortar matrix in the finished wall. The moisture content can be checked with a moisture meter. These are available for purchase at most building supply stores.

Having a volunteer list and a person(s) to call a 'work group' together when the need arose, was very, very helpful. The old adage, "Many hands make light work," was never truer when it came to peeling, cutting, splitting and stacking cordwood. It was not only a tiring day, but a good one since the work crew was varied in age, size and strength. Having a schedule of work times, rest times, break times, and lunch time is essential in maintaining a productive crew. Mixing the day with fun, laughter, and social activities makes the volunteers want to come back.

2.6 Even little ones got involved in stacking the cordwood log ends

2.7 Three 16 foot long stacks of cordwood look awfully good at days end. It is very important to brace and steady these rows. As spring approached and the ground heaved, ours tipped over a few times and had to be restacked

We used a borate spray on the log ends. Borate is an insecticide, a fungicide and a wood preservative; it does three things for the price of one. The log ends were sprayed with a mixture of 4 cups of 20 Mule Team Borax to a gallon of hot water. There are many different borate/borax wood preservative products on the market. The least expensive is either 20 Mule Team Borax from the store or borate ordered from a chemical store www.chemistrystore.com . We have also used Timbortm and Pentatreattm with success. Permachink's Shell Guard has propylene glycol that increases the penetration of the borate into the wood. Do a google search and see what works best for your budget. The main advantage of treating the wood, ahead of time is that it protects the log ends from insects, grubs or eggs that may have come along for the ride.

Keep the volunteers "hydrated" and well fed. If you want them to return, this project needs to have a "fun" component. Follow all safety rules and plan for the unexpected. When back in the woods it is imperative to plan for the worst case scenario. We always had a car pointed toward an exit road.

Portable Sawmills

If there is wood available on a building site, it is worthwhile to investigate how cost effective it will be to locate a portable sawmill to come and cut the timber into posts, beams and dimensional lumber.   At the Cordwood Education Center a portable sawmill owner volunteered to cut all the wood for the post and beam framework, the door frames, the window boxes and the interior and exterior siding.   The window box 2" x 8's and the siding were taken to be kiln dried and planed by local businesses. The post and beams were being stacked, "stickered," and air dried for a year and a half. (Stickers are 1" x 1" x 8' pieces of wood that are placed between the layers of wood to encourage air flow and facilitate drying).

Oftentimes unusual patterns and interesting knots will show up in timbers.   These add to the unique appearance of a hand-built structure.   The Wisconsin Woodland Owner's Association www.wwoa.org came to visit and the members remarked on how fitting a cordwood cabin could be for a woodlot owner.

2.8 The posts, window box frames ,ceiling boards, spruce slabs, paneling for the gable ends and keyways were cut on a portable sawmill. This helped save many dollars by cutting and using all the materials from the building site.

Many rural communities have individuals with portable sawmills. Finding one that will donate time (we paid for gas) is a worthwhile goal. If you have to pay for the portable sawmill hourly, factor that into your budget.

Chapter 3   Foundation

Foundation: Frank Lloyd Wright Style

The site was excavated for the foundation. A variation of the Frank Lloyd Wright style

*3.1 The rubble trench with a 4"
drain tile* sloping away *from
the foundation.*

foundation was chosen for its effectiveness in combating frost heaving. The foundation is prepared by scraping away all the organic matter from the site. Then an 18"gravel pad is dumped and packed on top of the subsoil.   A trench is dug around the perimeter of the foundation below the frost line (this is called a rubble trench).   Into the bottom of this trench a 4" drain tile is placed. The trench is then covered with large gravel all the way "to grade." The drain tile slopes away from the foundation. This encourages water flow away from the building. The 18" pad of gravel is extended over the rubble trench.   The idea herein, is that any water that might accumulate under or around the foundation and cause heaving, is eliminated with the gravel pad, rubble trench and drain tile. Frank Lloyd Wright called this a "rubble trench foundation" in his book, *The Natural House.* He used this foundation in his Wisconsin homes. It is now called a Frost Protected Shallow Foundation and is recommended by the NAHB (National Association of Home Builders www.nahb.com).

 Hire only professionals to do certain jobs.   Remember the old adage,
"You get what you pay for."

The Insulated Rubble Trench Foundation

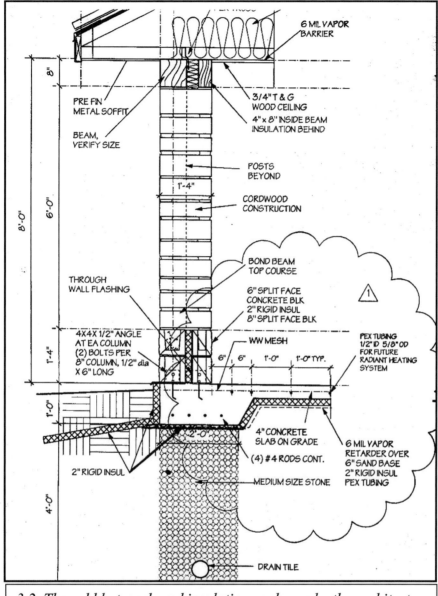

3.2 The rubble trench and insulation as drawn by the architect.

The foundation was then "squared up" and framed. It was insulated with 2 inches of extruded Styrofoam_tm underneath, on the sides and around the perimeter. All of the sheets of Styrofoam_tm were taped where they joined so as to not encourage an energy nosebleed to the soil below. This is an Energy Star_tm guideline. The rebar was positioned and fastened. Then two sections of 300 feet of ½ inch pex tubing were added for radiant in-floor heat. There will be a solar hot water/glycol system that delivers warmth to the slab.

The slab was poured and sealed. After it started to cure, it was covered with plastic. Finally in preparation for winter it was covered with bales of hay to insulate it from the cold and snow.

In spring the slab was cleared of the hay, swept and washed. The hay was placed on the soil around the perimeter to keep the mud at bay. It provided a spongy mat on which to walk, and was eventually raked to the side.

The slab made it through the winter in good condition. There was not a crack or heave. It is a testament to the careful preparation of the foundation site, the quality of the "pour," and the foresight to cover it during the freezing winter months.

3.3 Pex tubing, rebar and a drain cover.

Before pouring the slab, a floor drain was "stubbed in," two loops of pex-tubing, a toilet drain and electrical egress were all added. The planning stage is when a cabin owner or home builder would want to have planned all the necessary plumbing, heating and electrical inlets and outlets into the floor "before" the pour. It would be wise to consult with professionals so that an oversight (eg. a missed floor drain) would not occur that might be costly to correct.

⚡ One of the most critical parts of the whole process is having a good foundation. Consult with professionals to assure this is done correctly. The slab becomes both foundation and floor. Other foundations are certainly an option if a crawlspace or basement is desired.

3.4 The slab is covered with plastic and ready for winter.

Chapter 4

Winter preparation for cordwood infill

One very important part of the whole building process was to decide what could be done during the winter months. With volunteers asking to help, we set about organizing "winter tasks." Work days were set up to stain log ends, build bottle ends, clean log faces and stuff checks in the logs. One might also consider building cabinets, doors, furniture and any other jobs that would make the actual construction process go faster.

Here the log ends are being "cleaned." There are "hairs" or whiskers of wood that need to be taken off of the log ends. A Stanley Surform™ plane or shaver works very well on this job. One could also use a block with coarse sandpaper or a belt sander set up on a table stand.

The exterior side of the log ends are being stained with Permachink's Lifeline Exterior Stain. We used Light Natural (#120) on our log ends. This is basically a stain with a UV blocker. It is breathable, but should keep the log ends from darkening for many years.

4.1 Cleaning the "hairs" off the logs. A Stanley Surform™ shaver is used to remove any left over slivers after cutting the log ends to length.

4.2 Staining the exterior of the logends with Permachink Lifeline Exterior UV Blocker. This will help prevent the log end from darkening.

 Having a 'volunteer caller' to round up workday crews, is an invaluable part of a successful project.

Poor Man's Stained Glass Bottle Ends

One of the truly unique and interesting features of a cordwood cabin are the "things" that can be placed in the mortar. Stones, gems, antlers, footprints, and bottle ends are a few of the ways to make the cabin personal and unique.

Bottle ends are made from recycled colored glass bottles and clear bottles. Usually a wine or juice bottle provides the colored side and a canning jar or pickle jar provides the clear side. Commonly people will put the clear side on the outside and the colored bottle inside. When the sun hits the wall the bottle ends "light up." It is relatively easy to place them in random places as the wall rises, but there is also the option of making a pattern in the wall.

(See Big Dipper wall: page 41).

4.3 (Top to bottom) Bottle ends with aluminum tape, a handi-coil and clear packing tape.
Note that the bottle necks slide into the wide mouths of the canning jars.

The making of a bottle end is relatively easy. The picture shows a colored bottle and a clear

4.4 Bottle ends with objects inside.

bottle. The two are put together to equal the length of the cordwood wall, in this case 16"(notice that the neck of the colored bottle fits into the opening of the clear jar). Then the bottles are sealed together with aluminum duct tape, regular duct tape or an aluminum 'handi-coil.' Tiny holes are poked in the tape with a straight pin in order to help alleviate condensation that might develop. It is helpful to have two people when making bottle ends; one to hold the bottles in place and the other to tape them together.

The bottle ends must be washed with hot, soapy water and then dried. Cards, dice, and fishing bobbers have been placed inside the bottle ends. Children love to play "I-Spy" with these in the wall. Find something whimsical or that has meaning and put it in the wall.

Stuffing the Primary Check

The large diameter log ends have a tendency to develop a good size primary check. This check will oftentimes go from one end of the log to the other and, if not stuffed, allow air to flow to the

inside. Here two volunteers are happily filling the checks with non-formeldahyde white fiberglass insulation. The checks could also be stuffed with expanding foam (just don't let it seep out onto the log end face), or cellulose. This can also be done after the log ends have been mortared into the wall. If you wait until the building is completed then a wad of white fiberglass and a butter knife or thin screwdriver make an effective way to seal off this check. It is important to stuff the check on both the interior and exterior side of the log end.

4.5 Stuffing the primary check with white fiberglass. Sometimes this check will run all the way through the log end. Stuffing this check on both ends prevents air infiltration. Another option would be to use expanding foam to fill the primary check. However, with expanding foam, there is a "moment of truth", when the foam expands beyond the end of the check and onto the log face. Orange foam does not blend well with the log ends. If using this option, be very careful with the nozzle trigger on the foam can.

Notice the smiles on the faces of these volunteers. One of the biggest factors in making this project successful was the enjoyment of the community workers.

Chapter 5   Framing

Post and Beam Framework

The decision to build the center using a post and beam framework came for many reasons. For example, more of the sustainably harvested tamarack would be used in a post and beam framework, the rough timber framework offers a very attractive, appealing "look" to the building, and each 8' x 8' framed section made a manageable two day goal for cordwood infill. Having a framework in place would allow the roof to be erected and subsequently a dry work area would be established. Much of the finishing work could be started. The window boxes were built and installed, the electrical was "run" into the ceiling, the log ends could be brought inside and stained, stacked and kept dry before mortaring. Also, the Cordwood Center would be sitting open for quite a few months before the cordwood infill would begin (from May to September).

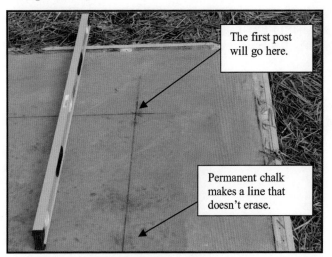

The first post will go here.

Permanent chalk makes a line that doesn't erase.

The framework would consist of two 7.5 inch tamarack posts (squared on three sides) and four 16" x 16" white pine corner posts, squared on two sides. The posts were left round where the round edge would be visible. This lends a natural, log cabin feeling to the building.

> 5.1 Before the first post can be positioned, the slab needs to be "squared up," so that all the posts will line up evenly. Therefore, an indelible chalk line is snapped, to create 90 degree angles for post and block placement.

Leveling the ends of the posts

After squaring up the foundation, it was time to put the posts in place.   These posts had been air drying for eighteen months. (The corner posts were squared on two sides and the side posts were squared on three sides). The corner posts go up first. Each corner post was cut on the interior two sides to form a right angle. This was done to make a flat surface for the cordwood infill to "butt up" against (see picture). The large corner posts make excellent "signature pieces" on the outside, but will not be seen on the inside of the building, since the cordwood will come right to the inside edge of the post.

4.2 Leveling the ends of the posts with a chainsaw.

Next a damp proof membrane, in this case "ice and water shield" was attached to the bottom of the post. This would make certain that no moisture could wick its way up the post. The membrane was then trimmed with a box cutter. One could use a shingle or rolled roofing for the damp proof membrane. The advantage to ice and water shield is that is has sticky tar on one side which makes it adhere to the bottom of the post.

4.3 Leveling the posts with a 16" Makita_{tm} saw.

Then the post is seated on the slab. It is squared, leveled and shimmed if necessary. This is the beginning of <u>checking and rechecking</u> everything for <u>level, plumb and square</u>. Measuring the hypotenuse of each rectangle will assure square corners and better "fits." This "double checking" time is well spent and assures that eventually the roof, windows and doors are installed "squarely."

4.4 Applying Ice & Water Shield

4.5 Keeping it level

Next the angle iron brackets are attached. They are held up against the post and the holes marked into the slab and post. The sleeve anchor holes are drilled with a masonry bit. The sleeve anchor is then hammered into the hole and the nut is threaded onto the bolt and tightened. It is important to have a shop-vac handy to suck the concrete dust "up" out of the hole.

Holes are then drilled into the post for the 4" lag bolts. The lag bolts are then tightened snugly with a ratchet. This gives the post lateral stability. It is a good idea to keep a level on the post as the bolts are being tightened so the post isn't drawn out of plumb.

4.6 Post brackets, sleeve anchors and lag bolts

4.7 *Drilling the pilot hole for the 4" lag bolts*

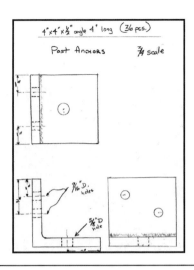

4.8 *Post anchor diagram* D. Wendorf

Squaring the ends of the posts

4.8 *Squaring the ends with a reciprocating saw*

In order to have the posts be level with the floor and top plates they were first trimmed with a reciprocating saw and then a skill saw.   The timbers were marked with a square on each side to insure an accurate cut.

The perimeter side timbers were placed in line, one at time.   Then they were notched on the top to accept the LVL (laminated veneer lumber). The LVL (which is engineered lumber) was then lag bolted to the notch in the post.

The posts for the perimeter walls were two 7.5" x 7.5" tamarack timbers. The timbers were squared on 3 sides, with the one side being left round. The posts were butted end for squared end.

Top plates and lag bolts

4.9 *Notching the top of the posts for the LVL*

4.9 Attaching lag bolts to the LVL.

The LVL's are lag bolted to the notched posts. Drilling pilot holes for the lag bolts helps to make a clean and smooth insertion of the bolts. In the picture, one person is drilling the pilot holes and the next person is drilling the lag bolts into the LVL with an electric drill with a socket attached to the drill.

The LVL's have to be checked for level and plumb as they are being attached, so the third person in the picture is eyeballing the whole process and using the level with every bolt. The adjustable wall brackets help with any variation that might occur.

The high school construction class volunteers had signed safety permission slips and came prepared with tool belts, safety glasses, hard hats and manners.

Safe scaffolding and attention to safety are crucial to the projects success.

Adjustable Wall Brackets

The red adjustable wall brackets are incredibly useful for keeping the building level and square. By simply turning the red portion of the jack right or left, the wall would be pushed 'in' or 'out' in small increments. This was extremely helpful in keeping the building square, especially when it came time to attach the trusses, door frames and window boxes.

4.10 & 4.11 Adjustable wall brackets are helpful in making adjustments to level & square.

The LVL's will be covered with a 2" thick spruce slab to give them a log "look."

The building is starting to take shape. The corner posts are up, the perimeter posts and the LVL's are attached. The truss bearing load is going to take place on the inside LVL's that run the length (34' 6") of the building. The two 7.5"x 7.5"s posts will make the width of the wall 16" for the cordwood infill. The top plates were leveled with a laser level that was set in the center of the slab. It was calibrated to the correct height of the interior walls (8'9").

4.12 The basic framing is in place. Leveled and double checked for accuracy by measuring the diagonal of the rectangle from corner to corner.

Once the framework was completed the crane was ordered to place the energy heel trusses in place. One of the many smart things the general contractor did was to sheet the gable ends with OSB sheeting and water shield on the ground, *before* the crane arrived. Then, rather than laboriously putting the siding up using ladders after the crane had left, the gable end siding was all in place with one lift of the crane's mighty arm.

Many volunteers are helpful at truss raising time: 6 to 8 is ideal.

Once again safety is critical, and the more experienced hands, the better, especially when high off the ground.

Good communication, hand signals and safety are of paramount importance when putting on the roof.

The gable ends were sheeted before being hoisted & attached to save time.

4.13 The crane makes it all so much easier.

The crane put the OSB sheeting on top of the roof. It was braced and it didn't have to be carried up by hand the next day.

4.14 The building framework is nearly complete.

Energy Heel Trusses

Once the trusses were up, the gable end ladder pads were built and secured. With a cordwood building it is a good idea to have large overhangs; at least 2 feet on each side. The exception is the east side where a 6' overhang was engineered into the truss to serve as a covered porch area. The energy heel part of this truss will allow insulation to be installed to R-53 in the ceiling. In another act of good sense, the roof OSB sheeting was placed (and braced) on top of the roof, with the cranes arm so we wouldn't have to haul it up by hand the next day!

The trusses were designed by API in Marshfield, Wisconsin. If you will look at the truss drawing, there is a 6' overhang designed into the truss. This clever feature gave us a 34'6" x 6' overhang porch to view the beaver pond. This means that we did not have to build a porch after the roof was up. This design feature could be incorporated on the opposite side as well. Another feature to notice is the energy heel portion of the truss; this is where the truss rests on the bearing plate. It is 14" high. Insulation can be placed in this truss so that portion where the truss rests on the top plate can also be filled with insulation equal to R-53 like the rest of the attic.

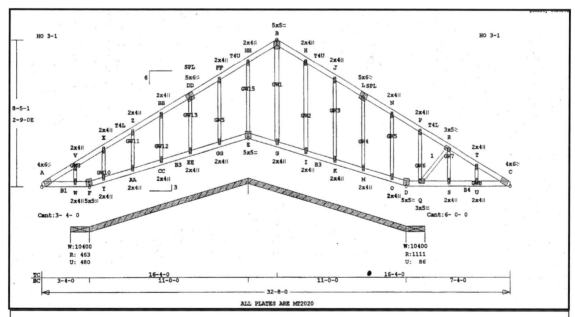

4.15 The energy heel trusses allow for maximum insulation at the bearing point of the truss. This truss has a 3/12 pitch on the ceiling and a 6/12 pitch on the roofline.

Top Plates and LVL's

To secure each truss to the LVL (top plate) hurricane ties were power nailed into place. The hurricane tie helps insure that strong winds will not have an easy time ripping off the roof or compromising the trusses or the post and beam framework.

4.16 A hurricane tie nailed in place.

The posts that are <u>not</u> on the corners are two 7.5" tamarack posts. These are set plumb and level with the outside line of the corner posts. There is a 2" gap between the posts which was filled with sawdust and lime insulation as the cordwood progressed.

Two 7.5" Tamarack posts, the center gap provides an insulation space.

4.17 The framework is complete.

There is also a "false" top plate on the outside of the long walls. The LVL bearing load was engineered for the inside wall and so the outside top plate had no bearing load. We used a "milled-on-site" 4" x 6" pine timber to fill that purpose.

The OSB was secured to the roof, water shield was placed over the roof and fastened and the building was enclosed from the elements.

The fascia boards were nailed to the end of the trusses in preparation for the soffit and fascia trim. A standing seam, brown metal roof was installed. Gutters were added so that all the water is carried away from the foundation. The building would now sit open for four months because the cordwood infill would not begin until the school year started on September 1.

Another advantage of having the post and beam framework in place and the roof completed, is that, if for any reason the cordwood infill could not be completed by winter, the 8' x 8' sections could be sheeted with boards, plastic or plywood and the building would be enclosed.

Funding is a very important part of the project. Donations, volunteer labor, donated materials and fund raising activities can help to overcome many obstacles

Window Boxes

A cordwood building requires that the windows be placed into a window box. The wall is so wide on a typical cordwood building (in this case 16" wide) that a window needs to have a framework so it can open and close.

The contractor made a template for the 22 window boxes that would have to be made of 2"x 8" tamarack. He built a 2"x 4" framework (or template) that would be the *inside* measurement of the window. Around that framework the window box framework would be attached.

This 2" x 4" will be placed diagonally and help brace the window box template.

Checking the diagonals.

4.18 Making the template for the window boxes.

Keeping it all level and square

In order to make certain that the windows would fit into the window boxes, the general contractor measured the hypotenuse of the template (see picture). This diagonal measurement should be exactly the same from the opposite corner.

The 2" x 8" tamarack boards were then cut to length, pilot holes were drilled and then screwed together to make a square window box. The corners of the window boxes were braced so they would stay square during construction.

4.19 The boards are pre-drilled and then screwed together.

The window boxes are hung; the outside one is first screwed with ledger bolts to the top plate. Then a 2" x 2" is placed under the window box to keep it level. Finally, the second window box is attached to the first window box and screwed to the inside top plate.

The outside window box is secured first. The inside box is screwed to the outside one.

A 2" x 2" is attached to the posts to secure the box.

4.20   The window boxes are "hung;" the outside one first, then the inside. A 2" x 2" is used to keep it all secured. Brace the window boxes so they stay square.

The Keyway Pieces

Vertically along each post, inside and out, a keyway piece is screwed to the post. The keyway is a code compliant device that mechanically holds the dried mortar so that wall isn't likely to tip.

Keyways

This was first devised for seismic regions, but it makes good sense to use it in all cordwood walls. It also acts as an air infiltration barrier. The keyways can be 1" x 1"or a 1" x 2".

4.21 Keyways along the post framework.

If you will notice, the block that has been laid in between the posts is actually two split face block. There is an 8" block on the outside and a 6" block on the inside. This leaves a 2" center cavity which is filled with 2" thick extruded Styrofoam$_{tm}$. The core of each block is then filled with white polystyrene$_{tm}$ beads.

This picture shows the block finished on all sides. The post in the foreground looks white because it has just been scraped and washed with a bleach and water solution. This was done to stop the mold that had developed from the pitch that the log oozed as it dried. The posts were then stained with a UV blocker from Permachink called

The corner post has been scraped and washed with bleach. It was then stained.

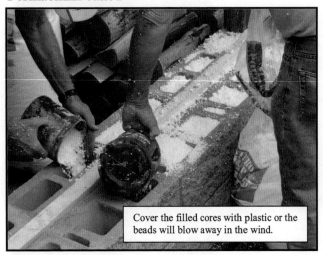

Cover the filled cores with plastic or the beads will blow away in the wind.

Lifeline Exterior Light Natural #120. All the exterior cordwood faces were likewise stained before they were mortared into a wall.

Here the block is being filled with polystyrene$_{tm}$ beads. It is very crucial to cover the top of the beads, or they will blow away with the first good wind. We cut a cover of plastic and stapled it to the posts.

4.22 Filling the block cores with polystyrene$_{tm}$ beads

Chapter 6   Cordwood Infill

Preparation for cordwood infill

There are many tasks that need to be completed before the cordwood infill can begin.   One is to clean the faces of the log ends if they have become darkened or dirty.

The pictured chop saw was used to clean up some of the smaller log faces for the inside of the building. The chop saw gave a clean, smooth face that was then stained on the outside (UV Blocker) and wiped with Murphy's Oil Soap on the inside.

(Note: a chop saw is a very powerful tool and is potentially dangerous if not used with safety in mind.)

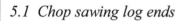

5.1 Chop sawing log ends

5.2 Cleaning and staining the log ends

5.3 Rounds were placed on top of the split-faced blocks (on the south and west side of the building) to help dry them out more completely.

5.4 Katy & Ryan are ready to mortar up the first wall at the Cordwood Center.

Mortaring Station

A good mortaring station "set up" can make all the difference between a long day and a very long day.

Here the mortar mixer is set up close to the building. The bags of Portland Cement and Hydrated Lime are to the right (Portland and Lime are taken, a bag at a time and placed between the sand the sawdust). Sand is in the middle and soaked sawdust is to the left. This way one does not have to move long distances to shovel the ingredients.

Each person will discover the most efficient placement of materials on their jobsite. Creating an effective "flow" of supplies and people is advantageous in conserving labor, saving personal energy and eliminating injuries.

5.5 Setting up a well planned mortaring station is one of the more important tasks in having a successful cordwood experience. Many steps can be saved and many extra hours of time can be properly directed at supplying the cordwood stackers.

Mortar Mix
3 parts sand
2 parts soaked sawdust
1 part Portland Cement
1 part Type S Hydrated Lime
(mortaring instructions page 83)

Crews of 5 to 7 volunteers helped to complete all the tasks involved with the cordwood infill. People are needed to mix mortar, prepare sawdust & lime insulation, position log ends, mortar log ends, clean up and get supplies. Plan the work well, too many volunteers lends itself to more socializing than working.

It was helpful to have many volunteers working on site to clean and prep the log ends. If one does not have access to extra help, the log ends will do just fine with careful planning and shielding from the rain and sun.

Many people have asked, "How did you accomplish this building project, when so many projects of this magnitude, fail?" Finding a 'lead person' or 'lead couple' to coordinate the activities is critical to the success of the project.

Beginning Cordwood Infill

It is helpful to protect the block, posts and floor from the mortar before starting. Since the mortar is put in place 'by hand' there is the potential for the mortar to get everywhere; the more surfaces that are protected, the better.

Falling mortar

When mortaring, mortar will naturally fall to the ground or floor. It is a good idea to put a piece of plastic on the floor or ground to catch the mortar. The mortar is then re-useable for short periods of time (approximately an hour) and can be rendered useful again with a little splash of water. When it crumbles, it is no longer suitable for use.
Plywood and cardboard have a tendency to rob the moisture from the mortar, but they can be used in a pinch.

6.1 The block is protected with plastic

When working with groups it is invaluable to have extra safety equipment handy. Gloves, masks, safety glasses, ear plugs are helpful in keeping the volunteers safe. Having a first aid kit and a cell phone on site is good planning. Water for the pooches is advised.

Wearing heavy duty rubber gloves (a gob of petroleum jelly is effective in protecting the skin), safety glasses and dust masks are all helpful in reducing injury and irritations. Lime and mortar can cause mortar burns on any exposed skin. When mixing mortar it is very important to not inhale the dust (use a dust mask). Knee pads on the floor and ground are a "must." Erect safe scaffolding when working near the top of the wall. Follow all building safety rules.

6.2 Two beads of mortar, sawdust insulation, a log end and a smile.

Starting a wall
The first beads of mortar are laid down (3" on each side). Using the two handed, "Plop & Stop" method works well to position the mortar into a continuous 3" bead. Using a Mortar Measuring Stick with the increments identified helps when starting cordwood infill or when instructing others in mortaring. The two mortar beads can be extended from one post to the other (approximately 8') and then insulation is placed in the center cavity. Next the first log ends are chosen and gently rocked into mortar bed.

Looking at each log end to see which side fits and looks best (outside and inside) is a crucial habit to develop. The clean face of the log end will go on the inside wall. The outside log faces have been stained with a UV blocker (Lifeline Exterior from Permachink) and this will reduce discoloration over the years. If working with two people, it is important to communicate how the log end looks on each side.

6.3 After the first row of logs is embedded, sawdust and lime are added to the center cavity. This is then tamped down to eliminate air spaces and potential settling. The cordwood chant goes like this: Mortar, Insulation, Log Ends, Repeat.

Tamping the sawdust/lime insulation with a stick.

Insulation 'poured in' with a 3 pound coffee can.

Tuck Pointing

Taking the time to tuck point at least twice is very important to the overall appearance of the cordwood wall. Spoons, butter knives (bent 30 degrees) and paint brushes can all be used effectively. Tuck pointing takes all the lines and fingerprints out of the mortar. A cup of water is handy to have to dip the spoon or tuck pointing tool into. It helps to make the joints smoother. A spray bottle is critical for cleaning log end faces and posts.

Tuck pointing is begun after approximately three rows (on an 8' run of log ends). The mortar is smoothed with the side of the hand, under and around the log end. This helps to firm the mortar and it actually strengthens the mortar bond.

Tuck pointing with the curved end of a plastic spoon.

6.4 Tuck pointing with a spoon.

In picture 6.4, the second round of tuck pointing is being done with the convex side of a plastic spoon. This is the final tuck pointing and helps to even out the mortar and find any gaps or bulges that may have occurred. This is the time to also take a good look at the posts, window boxes, bottle or rocks in the wall. Take time to clean and wipe them. If you look at the post in the picture you can see mortar stains. These posts should be cleaned by wiping them several times with a damp cloth. If the mortar dries, it will be much harder to remove.

It is a good idea to step back from the wall from time to time to make certain that one is not placing all log ends of the same diameter in the wall and to assure that the wall is looking "random." It is also helpful to eyeball the wall from the side and to ascertain how the wall is "looking." Now is the time to make adjustments, as once the mortar dries the wall is set.

6.5 Great Stuff foam™ with a contractor nozzle is an excellent way to fill under window boxes and top plates

When coming up to a window ledge or top plate it has been common practice to stuff fiberglass insulation in between the log ends, since there is no way to get sawdust in that gap. However, the general contractor on this project gave me a wonderful tip. Use Great Stuff Foam™ to fill the gap. It will expand and fill all the voids. In picture 6.5 a professional sprayer nozzle for the can of foam is being used. This nozzle can be used and will remain unclogged for six months, if it is cared for properly.

Special Effects: Footprints, gems, rocks

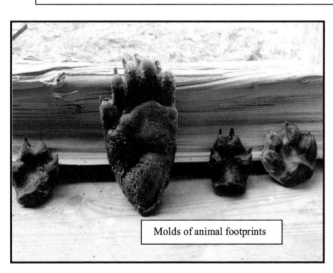

Molds of animal footprints

6.6 Animal tracks on a cordwood wall made with molds

The footprints in the picture were made from molds. The molds were placed in the wet mortar and tapped lightly with a hammer. The footprints can be made to follow a pretend trail

A coyote walked here!

on the wall. There is a turkey print on one wall that goes from bottom to top and looks like a turkey walked across the wall.

6.7 *Tapping a rock into a wall with a hammer*

Putting rocks, gems, fossils and stones into the wall is both easy and good looking. The wall should be partly "set up" or hardened, but not stiff. Take the rock, wet it, put it in place and then tap lightly with a hammer. This seats the rock in the wall. It may be necessary to pull some mortar under the rock/stone.

A few days after the wall is set up, if there is mortar on the rocks, stones and bottles, it is possible to go over the stones and rocks with Muriatic Acid. This acid is *very dangerous*, so follow all precautions on the label and wear safety equipment (gloves, goggles, mask, arm protection, etc.).

There is now a safer alternative to Muriatic Acid that is not as toxic. Check at the building supply store.

6.8 *Muriatic Acid is powerful, so please take safety precautions.*

Cutting pieces of log ends to fill "mortar joint gaps"

Having a good hatchet on hand to cut log ends to fit particular spaces is a good idea. In order to keep the face clean on each side, chop on top of a waste log end. Here you see a metal handled hatchet being driven with a 4 pound sledge hammer.

Start the split with the tap of a hammer. Put a piece of wood under the log end to keep it clean.

6.9 *A metal handled hatchet is very helpful in cutting log end pieces to fit a particular mortar joint.*

Mortaring in the sun

When the sun is shining on the mortar as the wall rises, it can quickly suck the moisture out of the mortar. One of the reasons soaked sawdust is used in the mix, is to slow down the set and cure of the mortar. Another helpful method of reducing the drying rays of the sun, is to "tarp" over the work area. Here a blue tarp has been screwed to the top plate with a 1" x 3" strip of wood. Then the ground portion of the tarp is secured with timbers, blocks, or anything heavy one might have around. The wind has a tendency to tear the tarp loose, so one needs to secure it firmly.

Keeping the wall level and plumb

The picture shows a device for keeping the wall level and plumb. It is a 1" x 4" hung on the top plate. This is done with a nail hammered into the top plate, after a hole has been drilled into the 1" x 4" and the board hung on the nail. This then freely pivots right and left and is good method of keeping the wall straight. Using a 6' level or an eight foot 2" x 4" are other ways to nudge the log ends to level and plumb.

6.10 A tarp keeps the sun off. The plumb stick keeps the log ends level.

Setting the Teeth & Filling the Teeth

When leaving a wall at the end of the day before tarping, it is wise to not place a mortar bead on top of the final row of log ends.   Leave the mortar so it comes to the side of the log end, but not above it. This is called "setting the teeth."
 If you need to work on the same wall the next day, simply wet the mortar and the log ends and proceed with mortaring. This is called "filling the teeth."

6.11 Setting the teeth

6.12 Ready to fill the teeth.

Mortaring over "cold joints"

If you have to leave a wall for a while and then come back and mortar, this is called mortaring a "cold joint." It is best to thoroughly wet the mortar (a paint brush and a pail of water works best) and the portions of the log end where mortar will be laid. This will prevent the mortar and the wood from sucking all the moisture away from the new mortar. If this precaution is not followed, it is not uncommon for the mortar to develop cracks as it pulls the moisture quickly out of the new mortar beads. Remember to use your mortar chant as you continue: "Mortar, Insulation, Log Ends, Repeat…"

Covering the walls

When finished mortaring for the day, it is critical to cover the work with plastic, blankets and/or tarps. These can be secured to the posts near them with a large staple gun. Boards can be placed over the plastic on the floor/ground. Conventional wisdom holds that mortar takes seven days to cure and 28 days to fully set. So it is a good rule to follow to cover the cordwood for seven days. This allows the moisture in the mortar to slowly dissipate. To reiterate, _cover the walls for 7 days._

End of the Day

It is a good idea to save an hour at the end of the day for final tuck pointing, clean up and covering the day's work. Covering machines, cleaning the mortar off wheelbarrows and tools also takes time and makes the next days start much easier. Cleaning the mortar from tools and machines is very important to keep them functioning. Picking up the debris that naturally occurs at a building site helps to eliminate trips, falls and unnecessary clutter.

Cleaning the wall

Clean the log ends with a wire brush after the cordwood has set for about a week. There is no possible way to keep all the mortar and lime off the log ends and the posts. It is good to clean up with damp cloths, as much as possible at the end of the day, but there is always some that sticks around. Once it has dried it can be removed by vigorously brushing with a wire brush.

Be sure to give credit to the volunteers. An article with pictures in the local newspaper, a bulletin board display, a website or blog entry that shows pictures, all helps to honor the people who are doing the work.

6.13 Cleaning the mortar with a wire brush

Chapter 7   Finishing up & Special Features

The building starts to take on a fortress-like finished look as the cordwood walls are completed one section at a time. It took 5 full weeks to complete the cordwood infill on this 24'6" x 34'6" building. Many times there were 3 to 5 people involved in mortaring on a daily basis. On the biggest workday "The Big Dipper Wall" there were 17 volunteers and 12 visitors.

7.1 The walls are finished!

Special Design Features

If considering a special design feature, this needs to be worked out ahead of time. For our "Big Dipper/North Star" wall we had an engineer (who also happened to be a volunteer) lay out the Big Dipper to scale on a large 8' x 8' piece of plastic. He used permanent magic marker. We stapled the plastic to the top plate and then rolled it up after we had marked the approximate height of the first bottle on the inside of one of the posts. As the wall rose to that height, we untied the plastic and unrolled it.   Then we were able to place the bottle end in the exact position.   The North Star (Polaris) comes off the cup of the front of the Big Dipper and can be a navigational aid and doubles as a teaching tool.   In the picture you will see the North Star if you follow a line off the front of the Big Dipper's cup. The song the slaves sang as they escaped from the south was "Follow the Drinking Gourd" i.e. The Big Dipper.

 Also in this picture you may notice a subtle "tree" in the wall. Look for the large round logs. There are six in the shape of a triangle and there is a tree trunk log on the bottom middle of the picture.

7.2 Big Dipper wall with subtle round log tree (find the 6 large round log ends and see the tree).

Cordwood siding

The electrical box had to take up so much room, that we could not put in full length cordwood log ends, but we wanted to maintain the look of the cordwood wall. What to do? "Cordwood siding to the rescue." Here the 1 inch discs of cordwood are screwed from the backside to a piece of plywood, to which chicken wire had been stapled. Then, with the board still on the ground we mortared in between the slices.

The advantage to this is that we could finish the small section of cordwood siding (3' x 4') on a

 set of sawhorses or a table. The mortar dried for an hour and then we screwed it to the 1" x 3" keyways we had attached to the post and beam framework. This wall had full length cordwood above and below the section of cordwood siding. Now, the only way to tell the difference between the two, is to tap on the log ends. The cordwood siding will have a hollow ring.

| 7.3 Cordwood siding before mortaring. Checking the "fit." | 7.4 Mortaring the cordwood siding on a table. |

A few builders have even done away with the mortar by painting the plywood a mortar color. If the cordwood discs had been recently cut and they were still green (meaning they will still shrink) this would be a good way to have the cordwood "appearance" without the mortar.

Cordwood siding is an effective way to keep the "look" of cordwood in a cordwood building. Sometimes there are situations where it is not feasible to mortar up full length cordwood logs. The long expanse above a sixteen foot garage door is a good example. The extra foot or so of space that is gained by using cordwood siding can be very important (like in a bathroom where space is at a premium). For those times, cordwood siding can be effectively used to keep the 'cordwood motif.' It is important to dry the cordwood discs well. Then it is your decision as to whether to use mortar or mortar paint for the background.

Windows

The windows and doors were donated for the Cordwood Center. The windows were donated by a local window products business that supports many community projects. The large windows were low-E, argon-filled casements that now provide good views of the surrounding woodland. Additionally they let in ample light for indoor daytime activities. The passive solar gain on the south and west side is also appreciated.

Window placement and sizing are major decisions when building. Take some time to draw frontal elevations of your project to see what the windows will look like outside and inside. As to the amount of square footage of windows, that is a consideration of local codes and personal preference. Some codes require at least 10% of the wall space be windows. The Cordwood Center was designed with plenty of light in mind. More than 20% of the wall space is window space. This makes the building bright and airy.

7.5 The windows fit into the window boxes from the outside. It is important to remember to brace the window boxes after mounting them in the structure. Often there is a period of time between attaching the window boxes and actually installing the windows. Bracing keeps the window boxes level and square. Caulk the window frames with a good quality caulk.

Doors

The doors were also donated by a generous local company that is very involved in the community. The doors have panic bars for the student's protection and safety glass. They are metal and match the warm brown trim pattern that was established. The business that donated them also was kind enough to do the installation.

Doors are another area where personal preference and resources come to the discussion table. Some folks like to make their own doors. Personally, we made two doors for my own home and are very pleased with how they look. One has a root for a handle and is 4.5 inches thick. The other has a pattern from an 18th century fort on Lake Michigan.

Just like with windows it is helpful to draw and experiment on paper with what is visually possible. If the door is to be an exterior door, insulation needs to be considered. In addition how much of the door will be glass?

7.6 These doors were generously donated.

183

Wood Stove & Heating

A local organization decided to make the Cordwood Center the recipient of a non-catalytic Vermont Castings Encore wood stove. This particular model is rated by the EPA to be the cleanest burning wood stove (0.7 grams per hour with 68% efficiency). The furnace company that ordered the stove also provided free shipping, a discount on the price, and storage of the stove until it could be installed.

HVAC and specifically heating or cooling the building is a matter of design, purpose and function of the structure. The Department of Energy offers a set of software called ResCheck™ that helps determine the heating needs of a building. Some states also use the ResCheck™ software for code compliance. Depending on the situation, it is wise to plan the heating and/or cooling system well in advance. Paying attention to Energy Star™ guidelines can make the building easier to heat and cool, by eliminating air leaks and design flaws.

The mat in front of the wood stove says, "Take a Hike!" That is exactly what the students are encouraged to do. It is a mile hike to the Cordwood Education Center, so it provides a means to that end. Notice the screens on each side of the stove. These are safety screens for young children.

7.7 *The Encore wood stove with a fire blazing and protective screen guards. This small stove heats the building to "toasty warm" even on the many below zero days we have during cold Wisconsin winters.*

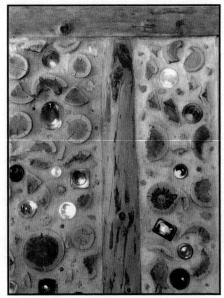

7.8 *One of the many beautiful walls with bottle ends, rocks and gems. In this picture the sun is shining through and lighting up the glass.*

A bright sunny winter's day at the Cordwood Education Center with sleigh rides offered by a local business.

Chapter 8   Best Practices & Energy Star™ Features

The building was insulated with cellulose in the roof and gable ends and softwood sawdust & hydrated lime in the cordwood center cavity. Every effort was made to build and insulate effectively. Every screw hole in the ceiling was taped over, every electrical outlet was foamed, the windows and doors were caulked inside and outside:

The Energy Star™ website suggests the following: "Building a green home means making environmentally-preferable and sustainable decisions throughout the building process-decisions that will minimize the environmental impact of the home while it is being built and over the many years it will be lived in."

A few of the outstanding Energy Star™ and 'Best Practice' features:

- 16" Post and Beam framework
- Frost Protected, Insulated Shallow Foundation (FPSF)
- Frank Lloyd Wright Style rubble trench
- Ceiling R-53
- Gable ends R-30
- Cordwood walls R-24
- Electrical outlets foamed
- Passive solar design
- Standing seam metal roof with snow brakes
- LargeThermal Mass
- Energy heel trusses
- High efficiency windows

- Permaculture/Naturescaping
- Solar photovoltaics
- Solar radiant in-floor heat
- Architecturally drawn plans
- State code approved building plan
- Volunteer built, donated materials, privately funded
- Sustainably-harvested materials

What are Energy Star™ Guidelines? Here is how the **Energy Star™** website defines its program to improve a home's efficiency. It is used, with permission, from their website. www.energystar.gov

Energy Star™ qualified homes can include a variety of 'tried-and-true' energy-efficient features that contribute to improved home quality and homeowner comfort, and to lower energy demand and reduced air pollution:

1. Effective Insulation

Properly installed and inspected insulation in floors, walls, and attics ensures even temperatures throughout the house, reduced energy use, and increased comfort.

2. High-Performance Windows

Energy-efficient windows employ advanced technologies, such as protective coatings and improved frames, to help keep heat in during winter and out during summer.

3. Tight Construction

Sealing holes and cracks in the home's "envelope" and in heating and cooling duct systems helps reduce drafts, moisture, dust, pollen, and noise. A tightly sealed home improves comfort and indoor air quality while reducing utility and maintenance.

4. Efficient Heating and Cooling Equipment

In addition to using less energy to operate, energy-efficient heating and cooling systems can be quieter, reduce indoor humidity, and improve the overall comfort of the home. When properly installed into a tightly sealed home, this equipment won't have to work so hard to heat and cool the home.

5. Efficient Products

Energy Star™ qualified homes may also be equipped with Energy Star™ qualified products — lighting fixtures, compact fluorescent bulbs, ventilation fans, and appliances, such as refrigerators, dishwashers, and washing machines.

Approximate cost:

To arrive at a realistic estimate of a final 'price point,' certain facts must be taken into account. Number one, much of the work was completed with volunteer labor. Secondly, the windows, doors, block and wood stove were all donated. With that in mind a general range of cost can be attempted, from a low end price to a high end. With those parameters, this 850 sq. ft. building would "cost out" at between $50,000 to $70,000 depending on how many portions can be completed with minimal cost and how much needs to be sub-contracted.

(Suggested) Tools to have on site:

rubber gloves	rags	camera
safety glasses	screwdriver	cell phone
work gloves	buckets	First Aid kit
wheelbarrows	sprayers	insect repellant
hoes	trash containers/bags	clock
hammer	water bottles	extra batteries
nails & screws	scissors	plastic bags
cordless drill	extra clothing	matches
staple gun/staples	tuck pointing tools	knee pads
dust masks	petroleum jelly	hatchet
ear plugs	rake	shovels
broom/dust pan	shop vac	extension cord
level	masons line	roll of plastic
plumb bob	ladder	paper & pencil
plastic coffee cans		

We actually put nails into the rough opening of the window box frames (after they were mounted) to hang some of the often needed supplies. It worked out very well as volunteers often went to the window box frames to get scissors, gloves, rags, and other needed supplies.

Becky made a batch of blue jean knee pads. She used the legs of blue jeans (the part from the knee on down) and stuffed them with old carpet pads (use whatever you have available). Then she sewed both ends together. They were a very handy knee cushion when working on the hard concrete floor or rocky ground.

Chapter 9 Renewable Energy

The Cordwood Education Center will have two main renewable energy features.

1. Solar Radiant In-floor heat with flat panel collectors.

2. Photovoltaic system with inverter and monitor controls.

This building was designed to model alternative construction techniques, using Energy Star$_{tm}$ guidelines and best practices. Early in planning it was decided to also make this a learning center for renewable energy. The community will have the opportunity to visit and study an off-grid building in the woods of northern Wisconsin. Since this is an area with many hunting shacks, cabins and cottages, the potential for renewable energy installations are enormous. Having the Midwest Renewable Energy Association (MREA the-mrea.org) just 50 miles to the south, we have access to some of the premier solar installers in the Midwest.

Radiant in-floor heat solar panels coupled with a 75 watt PV panel to run the DC pumps.

The committee worked to obtain funding for solar hot water radiant-in-floor-heat and a 1000 watt photovoltaic system with inverter and battery bank.

The solar thermal and PV system have been installed and are working well. So far we have installed.

- 75 watt Photovoltaic solar electricity system to run the heat pumps.

- Flat panel collectors for solar in-floor radiant heat system with Hartell DC pumps and potential drain off heat dissipation loop for summer.

The Midwest Renewable Energy Association (MREA) is good source for renewable energy information and hands-on installation workshops:
www.the-mrea.org

Chapter 10

How to "Go forth and do likewise"

Many people have asked if they could follow this example and build a bunkhouse, cabin or lodge for their camp, church, nature group or school system.

> ⚡ Look for the lightning bolt and text boxes like this one for hints on how to bring your groups project to fruition.

There are some basic tenants that led to the successful completion of the Cordwood Education Center and here is what we would suggest:

1. Establish a **Vision**. The initial idea was to build a small warming shelter for the students to stop at during their daily hike.

2. Allow the Vision to **evolve**. This warming hut evolved into a warming shelter, and then to an education center. It went from small to medium size. Finally, it went from a simple shelter to a best practices example of alternative construction and renewable energy.

3. Find a **benefactor and/or a fund raising mechanism**. This project was fortunate to have both: the support of a benefactor and also donations of eleven windows, two doors, the woodstove, all the block for the foundation and oodles of volunteer time.

4. Establish a **fund/budget**. How much will this project cost? Will you have a benefactor, donations or will you have to begin fund raising? This part of the process is important in establishing a set of monetary goals that will result in the completion of a successful project.

5. Finding an energetic **Core Group** of people to support the project is essential. When there are several people with the same goal/vision it becomes beneficial to split up the tasks so as to not overwhelm one person. For example, one person was in charge of calling volunteers, one in command of soliciting donations, another organized work days, etc.

6. Identify and employ the **Lead Person** (or lead couple). This is the person or couple who is responsible for planning the building and executing the plan: "Plan your build and build your plan." In this case, we became the Lead Couple and helped to organize everything from meeting with the architect, to scrounging bottles from the dump, to teaching cordwood construction techniques. This couple needs to have a good knowledge of building (but doesn't necessarily need to be the general contractor) and of the specific alternative construction style that will be used. (For example, in this case the Flatau's were proficient in cordwood construction techniques, having built a cordwood home, run cordwood workshops, written books and plans on the subject, and hosted the Cordwood Conference in 2005).

7. Make a **timeline**. The goal was to complete this project in two years: from planning to ribbon cutting ceremony. Success came, because everyone was working for a common goal;

The goal being to provide a beautiful model of alternative construction and renewable energy for the students of Merrill.

8. **Adjust the timeline** as needed.

9. **Keep everyone informed**. We worked with three different committees on this project, not including the School Board. This was logistically difficult at first, but became very helpful as each person's expertise was used in making difficult decisions. Keeping everyone informed made the process run more smoothly. This was especially important when planning a building for public use.

10. Realize there will be glitches and be ready to overcome personality differences. Be flexible. Listen.

11. **Involve the community**. Use personal contacts and the media to inform the community and to ask for help. The response was very satisfying and rewarding.

12. Realize that many **volunteers will be novices**.

13. **Use professionals** to make the building safe and well constructed. We used professionals to excavate, pour the foundation, blow in the roof insulation, build the framework, put on the roof, install the windows, run the wiring, etc. **Do not compromise with code issues.** They are there to make the building safe.

14. **Enjoy the process**. The School Forest Director started to use the building when it was safe, but not yet finished. Many students and parents had helped in the process. Others were delighted to witness the results of a community's labor.

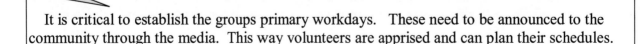

It is critical to establish the groups primary workdays. These need to be announced to the community through the media. This way volunteers are apprised and can plan their schedules.

Cordwood Stories

As each person builds with cordwood, new and better ways of doing things will be forthcoming. Jack was fond of saying, "Talk to the cordwood and it will answer." He means that intelligent people come up with their own solutions to problems with a modicum of reflection and searching.

In order that we may share with others, and if you would be so kind, please send me your cordwood stories, your tales of victory, failure and fulfillment. A few photos of your project would be greatly appreciated. If you would be willing to write a little narrative that would also be wonderful. At the next Cordwood Conference we will share these with other like-minded people. Thank you.

Websites of Interest

www.cordwoodconstruction.org	Richard & Becky Flatau's cordwood website
www.daycreek.com	The best cordwood forum, journal, photos, info
www.dirtcheapbuilder.com	Excellent online bookstore
www.taunton.com	Fine Homebuilding books
www.NAHB.com	Frost Protected Shallow Foundations
www.cordwoodmasonry.com	Rob & Jaki Roy's cordwood site
www.buildalt.com	Dr. Kris Dick's website
www.loghelp.com	Traditional log home products
www.backhomemagazine.com	Backhome magazine's website
www.motherearthnews.com	Mother Earth's website
www.naturalhomes.org	Excellent site on all things alternative building
www.permachink.com	Products for log cabins, caulking, log end treatment
www.sashco.com	Similar products to Perma Chink
www.nhla.com	National Harwood Lumber association (grading)
www.socketsys.com	New methods of using metal brackets for framing
www.thenauhaus.com	Clarke Snell & Tim Callahan digital book *Building Green*
www.aldoleopold.org/	Aldo Leopold Legacy Center
www.kubbhus.se/	Olle Hagman: Cordwood in Sweden
www.cc-cannon.net/	Clint & Cindy Cannon's cordwood/strawbale home: Manitoba

Cordwood Blogs

http://thisamazinghouse.com	Cordwood builders in NC
http://nerdwood.com	Cordwood builders in the UP of Michigan
http://survivingincivilization.com	Cordwood and commentary in Northern Wisconsin
http://home-n-stead.com/about/blog	Cordwood & Cob in the UP of Michigan
http://thecordstead.blogspot.com/	Sandy Clidaras beautiful cordwood home in Quebec
http://lightandliving.com	Bryan & Lois Pratt's gorgeous website on all things healthy
http://cordwoodgreenhouse.blogspot.com	Hannah Montana's cordwood greenhouse
http://thecordwoodonthepinewood.blogspot.com	Heather's cordwood project
http://sunny-wood.blogspot.com	Sun tempered, off-grid cordwood house in Maine

Recommended Reading List

Cordwood Construction: Best Practices 2012
W4837 Schulz Spur Dr., Merrill, WI 54452
715-212-2870
All the necessary information to build a cordwood dwelling.196 pages of color pictures, diagrams, line drawings, Formulas, mortar mixes, foundation options, best practices, mortgage free and up-to-date advice. with **Best Practices** as the theme 259 color photos. Richard Flatau
www.daycreek.com/flatau   www.cordwoodconstruction.org

Cordwood Building: State of the Art   2003
This handsome book is a 240 page volume, with contributions
from 25 different authors. It contains a wealth of valuable information about building a cordwood structure. It is a thorough and knowledgeable explanation of this earth friendly technique. Rob Roy www.cordwoodmasonry.com

Timber Framing for the Rest of Us
Describes the timber framing methods that use modern metal fasteners, special screws, and common sense building principles to accomplish a post and beam framework; This book includes everything an owner-builder needs to know about building strong and beautiful structural frames from heavy timbers. 176 pages, 120 B&W photos. Rob Roy

Foundations and Concrete Work, The Best of Fine Homebuilding, Taunton Press.
www.taunton.com Excellent source book on all types of foundations, including Frank Lloyd Wright's Rubble Trench Foundation.

Stackwall Construction: Double Wall Technique,
Cliff Shockey, Box 193, Vanscoy, SK, Canada S0L 3J0
Phone: 1-306-668-2141 Cliff's energy award winning double wall technique;
A delightful book loaded with excellent photos: very well written with "down-home appeal."
Also available from Cordwood Construction online bookstore.
www.daycreek.com   or   www.cordwoodconstruction.org

The Natural House: A Complete Guide to Healthy, *Energy-Efficient Environmental Homes*, by Daniel D. Chiras (Chelsea Green, 2000).Chapters on cordwood, strawbale, log, rammed earth, cob and adobe. 468 pages. www.naturalhouse.com

Stackwall: How to Build It, **by Dr. Kris Dick, PEng.**
Go to www.buildalt.com for ordering details.

Building Green by Clarke Snell & Tim Callahan   Lark Press (2005)
These two fine builders erected a beautiful cottage using cob, cordwood, strawbale, post and beam, living roof & earth plaster. They wrote a detailed book about it that contains 1500 color photos and 612 pages. If you are looking for which "wall building technique" to use, this book has them all).   www.nauhaus.com

10.1 Cordwood cottage in Montana (B & L Pratt).

Cordwood Construction: Best Practices   ebook $20 $25.00
                    2012
196 pages, 259 pictures, diagrams and formulas which take the novice
or experienced builder from house plans to occupancy. Sections include: mortar mixes,
new cordwood builder bios, types of wood, drying wood, shrinkage tables, how
we became mortgage-free, post & beam framing, formulas, insurance, Cordwood
Conference 2005 & 2011, Cob & Cordwood, Paper (and Cellulose) Enhanced Mortar, Permachink,
Building Codes, photo album, bottle ends, step by step: how-to "mortar-up" a cordwood wall, tuck
pointing, using mixers, weight of a cordwood wall, **Cordwood Education Center, Cordwood
Conference 2011, White Earth Cordwood Home, and much more.** *by Richard Flatau*
Cordwood Construction: Best Practices   **CD in PDF Format**   **$20.00**

  Special: *Cordwood Construction: Best Practices + House Plans*   **$29.00**

House Plans for Flatau's Chateau 1,624 sq.ft. Home   **$10.00**
 8 pages of plans include room dimensions, wiring, solar room (adds 400 sq.ft.)
deck, Room-in-the-attic trusses, slab, window & post placement, special foundation
details. These are detailed house plans on 11" x17" paper.
drawn by draftsman Rob Pichelman.
Cordwood Shed Plans   (Full Color)   **ebook $10**   **$10.00**
 Post & Plate structure, gravel foundation, built for
low cost per square foot, king-post trusses, ingenious
ladder-pad foundation. Build this first. 26 pages. This is a great way to
learn the cordwood masonry technique, gain valuable storage space, and
work out any mistakes. by Richard Flatau. **Our best seller.**
Cordwood Building: State of the Art   **$27.00**
by Rob Roy. This handsome book is a 240 page volume, with contributions
from 25 different authors. It contains 8 pages of color pictures and
contains a wealth of valuable information about building a cordwood structure.
Timber Framing for the Rest of Us   **$23.00**
Describes the timber framing methods that use modern metal fasteners, special screws,
and common sense building principles to accomplish a post and beam framework; This
book includes everything an owner-builder needs to know about building strong and
beautiful structural frames from heavy timbers. 176 pages, 120 B&W photos. Rob Roy

Cordwood Cabin: Best Practices   June 2009   **ebook $15**   **$15.00**
This all color book details the building of the Cordwood Education Center in
Merrill, Wisconsin. The building was designed to be green, use renewable
resources and model best practices with cordwood construction. It also explains how
a similar project can be implemented with groups. R & B Flatau

Cordwood Conference Papers 2005 or 2011   **ebook $18**   **$28.00**
27 fascinating articles from the Cordwood Conference 2005 & 2011
40 color photos, R-value testing from the U of Manitoba, Balewood,
Cordwood Dorm Room, Paper Enhanced Mortar, Log Prep & Foam Insulation,
Cordwood Siding, Engineer Built Cordwood, Recycling, Cordwood on a basement,
Frost Protected Shallow foundations, Bright and Airy & Pattern Language Cordwood, more.

Cordwood Conference Papers 2005 or 2011 CD   **ebook $20**   **$20.00**
  The Cordwood Conference Papers 2005 in CD format. All the photos are in
color. The Power Point Presentations made at the Conference are included and
so too are the complete, unabridged versions of all articles.

Cordwood and the Code: A Building Permit Guide + CD **ebook (no CD) $20**   **$26.00**
The first document ever published that deals specifically with Code Compliance
Issues. Included is 2005 R-value testing, Fire Resistance testing, certified
Compression tests, REScheck software explained, Building Permit samples & suggestions, A Sample
successful Building Permit Application Document, References, website and a CD of a sample building
permit document that you can cut, paste and modify to present to your code officials

   Books, CD's & ebooks can be ordered online at www.daycreek.com or cordwoodconstruction.org

Add **$4.00** postage (per book) for US orders (media mail)
           (Maximum $12 postage)
Add **$5.00** postage for Priority Mail (Total)
Add **$5.00** per BOOK ($2 for CD's) for Canadian orders

Mail to: **Make checks payable in US Funds to**:	*Richard Flatau*
Richard Flatau W4837 Schulz Spur Dr. Merrill, WI 54452	

Contact information: **Call or email if you have questions.**
 715-536-3195
 715-212-2870
 Flato@aol.com

www.daycreek.com/flatau

www.cordwoodconstruction.org

Ship to:
Name:_____
Address:_____
City, State, Zip_____

e-mail:_____**Phone:**_____

Index